MODERNIST DREAMS

BRUTALIST NIGHTMARES

LG THOMSON

www.Outcast-Press.com

(e-book) ASIN: B0BKRKD5HF

(print) ISBN-13: 978-1-7379829-7-5

This book is a memoir. The incidents it contains are described as I experienced them.

Names have been changed.

Everything else is the brutal truth.

Modernist Dreams Brutalist Nightmares
is dedicated to Joe

Author's Note

Most of us have made mistakes and done stupid or unpleasant things in our youth that we wouldn't dream of doing today and it is possible that someone who was a complete shit at the age of 12 or 14 is now an amazing person. While I have chosen to put this book into the public domain, I don't feel that it is right or fair to put other people's names out there even when I have only good things to say ('Joe,' I'm looking at you).

One of the many things I realised while writing was that—while some of my teachers were child-hating sadists who should never have been let loose in a classroom—most were not. The matter of whether a particular teacher is a force for good or a blight on humanity who makes it their mission to destroy the dreams of their young charges is a subjective matter.

They were trying to do their best for us and they deserve some recognition for that.

Especially my art teacher, Mr MacRae.

Map *of*

Chapter I.

Industrialised Violence

I'd like to tell you that I was born standing up and talking back but that would be a lie. The truth of me is that I was born being told to sit nice and play nice and, for fuck's sake, smile.

I didn't want to sit nice. I wanted to loll and sprawl and play in the dirt and make dens in the bushes. And I never did get the hang of playing nice which seemed to amount to me wearing a sick smile while the Boss Girl pointed out my flaws to the tune of the other girls' sniggers. My flaws, of which there were many, included my inability to play balls [1]and the shape of my face. Too square, the Boss Girl said.

My parents never swore in front of me. Not then. The fuck is mine, added for emphasis, a lie that tells the truth. Swearing wasn't the norm in my 1970s childhood world. *Bloody* was an occasionally overheard bad word, *fuck* was shocking. and I was almost of legal drinking age before I heard anyone say *cunt* out loud. Everyday words were weaponised in place of expletives. Girls were called *cow* and *boot*, neither meant as compliments. She wasn't tough as old boots, she was an UGLY BOOT, the hard consonants underlining the insult. Boys did not want to be labelled soft and nobody wanted to be called a swot.

Despite the expectation of smiles on demand, the threat of violence at home, at school and on the street was the norm. At school, teachers hit children across the palms of the hand with a leather strap called a tawse. The end of the tawse was split into tails which increased the sting while reducing the chances of drawing blood. Tawse production provided employment for saddlers and leather workers but, by the start

---

[1] A glossary of Scottish and British words is at the end of this book.

of the 1970s, demand for the leather straps was so great that high-tech machinery was specially designed to mass produce them. In Scotland, we industrialised the beating of our schoolchildren.

If you were given the belt by a teacher at school, chances were you'd be hit again at home for getting hit by the teacher. During one of his stand-up comedy routines, Billy Connolly told a story from his childhood about an adult saying to a child, *What are you crying for? I'll give you something to cry about.* He mimics using one hand to hold the child by the arm while using the other to beat the child on the backside, the slaps connecting with the small body in time with the words, *I'll-give-you-some-thing-to-cry-a-bout.* Connolly, who worked in the shipyards on the Clyde, reflected our lives back at us. The joke was funny because it was familiar and true—the words echoed at home. Do you want me to give you something to cry about? Well straighten your face then.

I was always being told to straighten my face. Did I not know how lucky I was? There were children starving in Africa and here we were with our nice wallpaper and wee plastic frames surrounding the light switches to save the nice wallpaper being marked by greasy fingers.

YOU DON'T KNOW HOW LUCKY YOU ARE.

When I was in trouble at home, my father threatened to leather my backside with a thick, black belt he called Rastus. Rastus lived in the wardrobe in my parents' bedroom. I was shit scared of Rastus.

While my father threatened me with Rastus, my mother threatened me with my father. *Wait until your father gets home* or *Wait until your father hears about this.* You couldn't escape it. You could be outside playing and some kid whose name you didn't even know would say, *Your da's looking for you*, and you knew you were in trouble. I'd walk home, dragging my feet, trying to delay the inevitable. Other times, I'd be getting home pronto, hiding in my bedroom because some kid said they were going to tell their maw on me or that their da was bigger than my da and their da would batter my da or they were going to get their pal's big brother to batter me. I was shit scared of many things. Rastus, other people's big brothers, other people's big sisters, getting into trouble at school, wasps, bees, falling off high things I shouldn't have been on, that family at the end of the street with the fancy red car and permanent scowls. But most of all, I was scared of being battered.

For every battering that ever happened, there were hundreds of threats that came to nothing but that didn't lessen the heart-thudding impact of being told that you were going to be got. This man told my father that he was going to get him. I only found out about it when the police came to our house. Nothing much exciting happened in our street, so a police car parked outside our front door was pretty conspicuous. The other kids stared at me and later the Boss Girl said, *I saw the police at your house.* She said it like an accusation. I was annoyed about that, but I was more annoyed that she knew as much about it as I did. My parents had this rule about not telling me stuff that might have been useful or interesting or just good to know. People came to visit, and I knew I was related to them somehow, but without being told so directly, I knew I wasn't allowed to ask. Sometimes I felt pretty stupid because of the things they never told me.

I wasn't allowed in the house when the police came. Seeing them arrive was thrilling and terrifying at the same time. I tried to wander in behind them, but my mother told me to go and play. They probably didn't want to tell me anything at all but with it all being so out there and obvious, they had to tell me something.

The man who was going to batter my dad followed him out of the pub and my dad hit him over the head with a lemonade bottle. My dad was bringing the lemonade home for my mum's whisky. She drank it really diluted so that it lost its golden colour. Whisky shandy, my dad called it. The way I heard it, even though my dad was the one doing the hitting, the other man was in the wrong and the police must have thought so too because that was the end of the story. The only time the police came to the house after that was when they caught my sister underage drinking and took her home. I'd left by then, but my sister told me my dad went mental and pushed her, and her head banged against the wall. It made me pretty glad the police had never caught me drinking.

When I was at primary school and two boys wanted to fight each other, they'd say, *See you at the back of the Mungo.* St Mungo's, named after the patron saint of Glasgow, was the church next to our school. Though I was unaware of it at the time, the church's design, with its impressive pyramidical roof thrusting towards the heavens, encapsulated the modernist vision for Cumbernauld. This was counter-balanced by the utilitarian cross that looked as though it had been made from girders in a Govan shipyard before being planted in front of the church.

Before the tax office was built, there was a big field at the back of St Mungo's where we gathered to watch the fights. They didn't happen that often, so when they did, it was a big deal. You could hear the buzz going around the playground and whispered in the classroom—*Fight after school, fight after school.* We were like sharks getting the scent of blood. But while we were working ourselves into a frenzy over the possibility of watching two boys knocking lumps out of each other, the fighters would experience a change of heart, their anger evaporating by the time the last bell went, but, by then, it was too late to back down.

The crowd circled around the reluctant fighters, everyone jostling for the best view while the two boys faced each other, with neither wanting to throw the first punch and both just wanting to run home. There was jeering and tension and we shouted, *FIGHT FIGHT FIGHT!* Then someone pushed one boy towards the other and someone else pushed the other boy towards him and then they'd be on each other, scrapping like dogs, and we'd be chanting, *OH-OH-OH-OH*, and then someone would yell that the janny was coming and everyone scarpered.

Mostly I went to school dinners[2] but one day I went home for lunch and, right outside my house, two men were

---

[2] Even although we might go home for lunch, the mid-day meal was always referred to as school dinners. Our evening meal was usually between 5.30 and 6pm and was called our tea.

kicking holy shit out of another man who was lying on the ground, trying to protect his head with his arms. They were older teenagers but I was a little kid, seven or eight, and they looked like men to me, tall and dangerous, wearing bomber jackets and parallel trousers and clunky shoes that must have felt like bricks when they were pounding into his body.

I ran into the house and told my mother and she came out and yelled at them to leave him alone. They gave him another couple of kicks before running away. My mother asked him if he was okay and, even though he was all bashed up, he said yes and off he limped.

I had a bowl of Heinz Cream of Tomato Soup for lunch and, on my way back to school, I stopped to look at where the kicking had taken place. You'd have thought that something so vivid and visceral would leave a trace of itself but there wasn't even a drop of blood. Nothing but grey road.

We lived in a culture of blame, and I wondered what the one on the ground had done to make the other two want to batter him. I don't suppose he knew any more than I did that we were doing our growing up in the safest town in Britain.

Meal footnote continued: If we ate later on, that was supper. Supper in our house was a light snack comprised of a slice of toast or semi-sweet dry biscuit (cookie), taken with a cup of tea, hot chocolate, or milk. There is also High Tea, which in Scotland was served between 4 and 6.30pm and consisted of a normal dinner such as fish and chips or gammon steak, along with toast and a big pot of tea, followed by a selection of dainty cakes and pastries served from a tiered stand. I only ever experienced High Tea as a rare holiday treat.

Chapter II.

Earliest Memories of a Bad Girl

I was born in Glasgow in 1964. Manfred Mann were at number one in the charts with "Do Wah Diddy Diddy" and the Beatles, the Beachboys, Billy Fury, and Dusty Springfield were all in the top ten. The biggest film releases that year were *Mary Poppins, My Fair Lady*, and *Goldfinger*. In the news, mods clashed with rockers on Britain's beaches, Cassius Clay became the heavyweight champion of the world, Nelson Mandela was sentenced to life imprisonment on Robben Island, and, although nobody knew it at the time, it was the last year that the UK would send anyone to the gallows.

My first home was a single end in Bedley Street, Springburn, in the north of the city. A single end was a one-room flat with a bed recess and a communal toilet on the landing. There were only the three of us in ours but, across Glasgow, it was common for large and/or multigenerational families to live in single ends.

Springburn began as a rural weaving community but, with the opening of its railway station on the Glasgow–Edinburgh line in 1842, it underwent rapid expansion. 30 years later, it was incorporated into the city of Glasgow and, by the start of the 20th century, masses of tenements had been built to house the 30,000 inhabitants of the one-time hamlet. In 1904, the local poorhouse was expanded to become the largest in Scotland. Inmates earned their keep by separating tarred rope fibres (known as picking oakum), breaking rocks, and making up bundles of firewood. If they didn't reach their quota, they were put on a bread and water diet and locked in solitary confinement.

The slum tenements and Barnhill poorhouse reeked like a Dickensian hangover, but I don't remember any of that on account of it all happening before I was born. My only memories of living in Springburn are shadows embellished by a few black and white photographs, fattened by stories my parents told me. Like how my dad was so proud when I was born that he wouldn't let my mum push my pram through puddles, and about the time my dad was walking past a phone box with his granny-in-law and the phone rang. My dad went in to answer the phone and saw a bottle of whisky sitting on the shelf, so he nabbed it and showed it to Old Maw, and the pair of them high-tailed it back to Bedley Street. They cracked out the glasses, but it turned out to be a bottle of piss, the whole thing a set-up by some prankster.

Then there was the time the man who lived upstairs invited my parents up for a drink. He had a room full of people and a piano and my dad started boasting about how well my mum could play and she said *no, no*, and the neighbour thought it was false modesty and insisted she give them a tune, so my mum sat at the piano and everyone gathered around to listen to her playing "Chopsticks." And then there was another time when my mum heard a cow lowing in the back courts and she couldn't understand what a cow was doing down there but it turned out that a man had been stabbed and the sound was him moaning as he died.

My first actual memory that's all mine is of a woman hitting me with a small boy. I know it's a real memory because no-one was there to tell me about it happening. My dad was at sea in the Merchant Navy, my mum was in hospital, waiting to give birth to my sister and my auntie, who I was staying with, was at work.

The woman hauled the boy towards me by the arm and, when he refused to beat me on her command, she raised his hand by the wrist and did the job for him. Each limp slap was accompanied by the words, *Bad girl, bad girl*. I was being punished for skipping ahead of him in the queue for the wooden slide. Despite her efforts, his tiny hand didn't generate much in the way of pain but, as my chastisement was meted out in a room full of people who were staring at me, the humiliation was acute. My earliest memory is shame.

It was December 1968 and I was in Govan, in the creche of the factory where my auntie worked. She lived with my uncle and cousin in a tenement at Govan Cross. Any further memories I have of staying with them have soaked into the many memories of visits over the years. I liked visiting relatives in general because there was a good chance I'd get a biscuit or a packet of sweets, but going to my auntie's house was particularly good, as I would see my cousin. He was a year older than me and I was wildly jealous of a poster he had on his bedroom wall of Christopher Lee as Dracula.

They lived on the top floor and the stairs were still lit by grimy yellow gaslight, as they would have been when the tenement was built in the 19th century, back when Govan was a town in its own right, looking across at the city of Glasgow from the south side of the River Clyde. At the top of the building, the stairs spiralled around a central column as they did in medieval towers and, though they were made of stone, the steps bevelled in the middle, worn by the tread of footsteps over many decades.

There was an acoustic guitar hanging on their living room wall, alongside a replica of the kind of rifle you'd see in cowboy films. My uncle carved the rifle out of wood, painting the barrel black to make it look like the real thing. They were big country and western fans and had a framed picture of the singer Hank Williams Sr. They had a lot of parties where my uncle played the guitar and my auntie sang songs like Hank Snow's "Yellow Roses." It seemed to me that all the country and western singers were called Hank.

One time when we were visiting them and my mum and dad and my auntie and uncle were having a few drinks and singing a few songs, my dad tore off a strip of newspaper and held it at the electric fire.

My auntie stared at him and then asked, *Do you want to tear paper?*

I'm just lighting my cigarette, my dad said.

You want to tear paper? she repeated and then picked up the newspaper and tore it into shreds. *You want to tear paper, eh? Eh?*

While this strange exchange was taking place, I was in the back room with my cousin, the two of us jammed into an armchair, eating a box of Ritz crackers while we watched an old horror film on the telly.

All of this singing and tearing up paper and munching on crackers took place only a 10-minute walk from the shipyard where my uncle worked. In their heyday before the First World War, the yards employed over 70,000 people to build navy vessels, steamers and luxury ocean going liners. Ships built at Govan's Fairfields yard won the Blue Riband, an unofficial honour for crossing the Atlantic in the fastest time. To say a ship was Clyde-built meant that it was world class, but, by the time my uncle was there, the workforce was down to 8,500. The decline began after the Second World War and dribbled on until Maggie Thatcher[3] (prime minister of the UK and generally loathed in Scotland) destroyed most of what was left of the industry in 1988, selling off the scraps to the Norwegian Kvaerner group.

My uncle's yard was already long gone by then, having shut down without notice in the late 1970s, making thousands of men instantly redundant. It was a desperate time, and he wore out his shoes walking the streets, often for eight hours at a time, looking for a job. He finally found one as a security guard. The money wasn't anywhere near as good as he'd earned as an engineer in the yards, but it was a job.

Their flat had an inside WC (wash closet) with a toilet and hand basin but no bath. There was my cousin's bedroom, the living room, and the back room where my auntie and uncle slept on a zed-bed that was folded down every night and folded back up every morning. The room overlooked the back courts where children played and rats ran in the middens.

---

[3] I only ever heard her referred to as Thatcher or Maggie, never Margaret. On protest marches the chant went, *Maggie, Maggie, Maggie, out, out, out. Maggie. Out. Maggie. Out. Maggie, Maggie, Maggie, out, out, out.*

There was a tiny scullery off the back room containing a cooker and sink. It was too small for a door so was separated from the main room by a curtain made of brightly coloured plastic strips. I was frequently told off for twirling myself in the long strands, pretending they were my hair or a fancy dress.

My auntie and uncle had a tank of angel fish. These were the most beautiful creatures I'd ever seen and I'd sit and watch them for minutes on end. Even though they didn't have a bathroom or even a proper bedroom, between the plastic strip curtain, the angel fish, and my cousin's *Dracula* poster, it seemed to me that my auntie and uncle had all the good stuff.

They even looked exciting. My uncle had a quiff and wore bootlace ties and my auntie had waist-length black hair and long, red nails. She wore red lipstick and a shitload of eyeliner and mascara. The first time I saw her without her makeup on was a strange experience. Her face looked bald. I yelped, then had to pretend I was coughing. She usually dressed in black and wafted about the place like Govan's very own version of Morticia Addams.

It was a time of change in Glasgow. There were wastelands all over the city as the old tenements were bulldozed and cleared. Within a few years of the woman in the creche beating me with the small boy, my auntie's tenement was torn down to make way for a shopping centre. The ghost of her flat now hovers above a branch of Greggs[4]. My auntie and uncle moved to a new housing development overlooking the Clyde, not far from where my Great Uncle John's body was once upon a time recovered from the river. Meanwhile, we had moved to the Town for Tomorrow.

---

[4] A bakery with branches across the UK, serving sweet and savoury pastries, sandwiches, coffee and other drinks. Greggs specialises in affordable, hot take-away food, such as steak bakes and their utterly delicious vegan sausage rolls.

Chapter III. 🍨 The Toonie

During the Second World War, Scotland endured over 500 air raids by the Luftwaffe, the worst being the Clydebank Blitz in March 1941. John Brown's shipyard and the Singer Corporation factory, which had switched from making sewing machines to fulfilling government weapons contracts, made Clydebank a target for over 1,000 bombs. Over two nights, 528 people were killed and another 617 seriously injured. The catastrophic attack left only seven homes in the town undamaged and rendered more than 35,000 people homeless. Two months later, downriver at the Firth of Clyde, the Greenock shipyards were targeted. An intense night-time bombing campaign killed 271 people and injured over 10,000. 5,000 homes were destroyed and another 25,000 damaged.

Though Clydebank and Greenock suffered the worst of the bombing, further up the Clyde, Glasgow was not unscathed. Bombs were dropped at random and, by the time the war was over, Glasgow was facing an acute housing shortage. Undestroyed homes became slums. A solution was the conception of Scotland's five New Towns. The most ambitious of these was Cumbernauld. Development began in the late '50s and, by 1968, my family were New Town pioneers.

A geometric city built on a hill served as the beating heart at the centre of my new hometown. The shapes and angles of the grey colossus were constructed from a brutalist network of poured concrete. To walk inside Cumbernauld Town Centre was to enter an Escheresque landscape of bridges and ramps, galleries and stairs, vast concourses, and labyrinth malls lined with a cornucopia of shops, pubs, and offices. On the top level: the penthouse flats, the town hall and the library. Hidden beneath: car parks, the bus station, and a modern health centre.

Known locally as the toonie[5], this megastructure was Britain's first indoor shopping mall. Orbited by a network of neighbourhoods, the toonie housed the entire social, business, and recreational needs of the population. It was the focal point of the New Town and all paths led here.

The external aspects of the geometric city were not uniform and each of the neighbourhoods it served were presented with a different façade. How it looked to someone from Carbrain was entirely different to the view from Seafar or Kildrum. It was so huge and disparate a construction, it was impossible to experience it as a whole. Each part and layer was a unique sensation. One moment, you were in an artificially lit mall with gaudy illuminated shop signs and sparkling window displays. Seconds later, you could be on a rooftop terrace, the tang of vinegar in the air as someone walked by with a bag of chips from the Abetone, while on the library level, the sun shining through a glass roof lent an otherworldly feel to the futuristic shapes and modernist angles.

Rules and regulations were different back in the day and helicopter parenting hadn't been invented. From a young age, you walked to school by yourself and, out of school hours, you were mostly left to your own devices. You'd go out in the morning and free range it until you were hungry or you heard word on the street that your mum or dad were looking for you, either because your tea (evening meal) was ready or because you were in trouble. Or both. By the time I was 10, I was picking my sister up from the childminder on my way home from school to look after her until either of our parents came from work. In later years, while narking at me for encouraging independence in my own kids, my parents denied this happened. It happened and it was normal. Just about every kid I knew had a parent-free gap at home between the final school bell and the end of the parents' work shift.

After school, we mostly watched telly but, on occasion, I'd go wandering with my sister and, on the rare occasions we

---

[5] Toonie – a contraction of Town Centre. This shortening is typical in Scotland, e.g., a chip shop known as the chippy, headmaster becomes the heidie, a bookmakers (licensed betting shops) are bookies.

had money, we'd go to the toonie and visit the milk bar in Galbraith's supermarket. There we sat, side-by-side on high stools at the long counter, feeling all grown up as we sipped strawberry milkshakes from tall glasses through paper straws.

Across from Galbraith's was an open-air terrace always crowded with kids where you could hire a bike and ride around a circuit painted with road markings. Mothers often dumped their kids there while they went off to get the messages[6] but my mum mostly took me to the shops. This inevitably meant a trip to Galloway's, the butcher. I hated the smell of the meat but loved to hunker down and play with the sawdust on the floor.

Stop that, Lorraine, you'll get dust in your eyes.

The command was repeated several times on every visit until I inevitably got dust in my eyes, but the draw of the powdered wood was irresistible. My mother's words floated over my head while I scooped the bloodied sawdust into mounds and let it flitter between my fingers like fairy dust.

Next door to Galloway's was the City Bakeries with its much more appealing smell. I'd occasionally be treated to a fern cake or an empire biscuit and my mum bought a half dozen well-fired rolls. Well-fired being what other people might refer to as burnt.

Years after I'd stopped playing with the butcher's sawdust, I was sent to the City Bakeries to buy a French stick (what we now call a baguette). The end of the loaf was sticking out of the paper bag and so I broke off a piece and chewed it on the way home, thinking passers-by would consider me highly sophisticated and *très continental* rather than a daft lassie chewing a lump of bread in the street. My mother wasn't too chuffed when I presented her with the gnawed loaf.

There was always a lovely smell of coffee in the Scan bookshop accompanied by the *chink* of glass cups and the hum of conversation from the café upstairs, but the best smelling shop in the toonie was by far the Vineyard. Cloaked in the aroma of freshly roasted coffee beans, the Vineyard was also the toonie's most sophisticated shop. As well as selling fancy

---

[6] Shopping, groceries.

coffee, they sold sherry from barrels along with all sorts of other exotic delicacies we never bought.

The only person I knew who drank sherry was a man my father worked with. The sherry-drinker favoured a cheap brand called Emva Cream. One of the other factory workers found out about this and, as cheap sherry was seen as the preserve of those who couldn't afford whisky, he started referring to him at work in a sneering way as *Emva*. My dad got wind of this and gave the name-caller a sherricking. The name-caller laid off and Emva, whose name was Allastair MacDoug, became friendly with my dad, and then he and his wife Margo became friendly with my mum and, before you knew it, my sister and I were calling them auntie and uncle and they were at our house the next 16 Christmases.

When I was a little kid, one of my favourite shops in the toonie was Kay's hardware store. The wooden banister on the steep staircase leading down to the basement was inlaid with big copper pennies that every kid in Cumbernauld tried to prise out on the way down. No-one ever succeeded.

Across from Kay's, RS McColl's sold sweets by the quarter-pound and, if you couldn't afford that, they'd sell you two ounces. Even a two-ounce bag contained hundreds of Tom Thumb Pips. These were tiny, round, hard-boiled sweets. At school, there was a craze for using pen casings like pea shooters to blow out Tom Thumb Pips like missiles. The teachers flipped out at the prospect of someone's eye being taken out and Tom Thumbs were added to the banned list along with Space Dust[7].

Everyone went nuts for Space Dust when it came out. It was like fireworks going off on your tongue. We poured entire packets into our mouths and listened to the candy frizzling and cracking inside each other's skulls. My pal gave some to her cat and nearly had a seizure laughing when the cat lost the head[8] and started fighting with itself. Then a rumour went around that some kid's head exploded after he ate too much Space

---

[7] The US equivalent being Pop Rocks
[8] "To lose the head/heid" means to lose control of one's temper.

Dust at once and they banned it just the way they banned Tom Thumb Pips and all the good things, like clackers.

Clackers were a toy comprising two hard balls on either end of a string that you clacked against each other. Being good at clackers was the same as being good at the yo-yo—you could do tricks and spin them around and clack them above your head and all the while they'd be making this *clack clack clack* sound. My lousy eye–hand coordination meant that I was never any good at it, but I once watched an older girl work them like a pro. And then some kid got their jaw dislocated by a clacker and all the clackers were disappeared.

I knew about the Tom Thumb Pips because the pea shooting thing was happening in my class, but I didn't really believe the story about the kid's head exploding because of Space Dust, same as I didn't believe the story about the girl in Cumbernauld who tripped over her flares. When she stumbled, the pencil she was carrying went through her eye and damaged her brain, but then I went to high school and that actual girl and that made me wonder if Space Dust actually made a kid's head explode.

The toonie had a Market Hall and in the Market Hall there was Larry's Record Bar where my pal Joe would one day buy a copy of Elvis Costello's *Armed Forces*, and there was a fruit stall where you could buy chipped apples for a cheaper price and a shoe shop that sold Jesus sandals, because this was the 1970s and they were all the rage.

There came a time when I felt worldly buying Bombay Mix from the wholefood stall, thinking I was sophisticated for eating spiced fried lentils instead of a bag of prawn cocktail Skips, but I never did go into the Wimpy that was just outside the Market Hall. It was somewhere my mother never went and, by the time I could afford to take myself, I was too intimidated to walk into the burger bar with its busy window seats and people who looked like they belonged. I was too shy by far to go in and order the Brown Derby doughnut and ice-cream concoction I'd desired for so long.

I had no such reservations about going into the rooftop Abetone chippy on my way home from the swimming pool and, if I was feeling flush, I'd get a pickled onion to go with my chips. Along from the Abetone, was Retson's, the hairdresser's where one day, when perms were all the rage, I would go in and ask for a loose, shaggy perm and come out looking like Hair Bear from the *Hair Bear Bunch* cartoon. I didn't get it cut for months afterwards and ended up with a giant halo of hair.

The toonie was where I bought my first single, *Daddy Cool* by Darts, and my first album, Blondie's *Parallel Lines*. It was where I went along with hundreds of other kids for Uncle Bob's Saturday morning picture shows. The toonie was where I bought *Little Old Mrs Pepperpot* books by Alf Prøysen, and later stocked up with horror books by James Herbert, Stephen King and Ira Levin. It was where I bought my first underage alcohol and also the cough mixture I drank to get high.

The toonie itself started on a high. Initially regarded as an innovative and significant moment in urban design, it was internationally acclaimed as a star in the firmament of brutalist architecture. Bold, stark and brutal, the toonie was a place like no other, but, in the following decades, Cumbernauld town centre was lambasted and derided, winning the Carbuncle Award[9] for Scotland's worst town centre twice over.

The full vision for the toonie's development was never realised. A design flaw meant that it was effectively a giant wind tunnel, while, beyond its fortress walls, a generic retail park was developed and lay siege. The shoppers were drawn away, rendering the toonie a concrete ghost town populated by little more than discount stores and charity shops. Once a ground-breaking concept in community living, the toonie became a metaphor for broken dreams.

But all of that came later. This tale is set in the 1970s when life in the New Town was still an exciting prospect. The air was scented by dog roses and optimism, and one third of the population was under the age of 15.

---

[9] Tongue-in-cheek prizes awarded by Scottish magazine *Urban Realm* for bad architecture with the aim of provoking public discourse.

Chapter IV. 🌺 Concrete Pipe Dreams

In a time of monumental change, we were shipped to the New Town from another place, a different era. Moving from a one-room tenement flat with a shared outside toilet to a three-bedroom modern flat was like stepping over the rainbow from grainy, black-and-white kitchen-sink drama to glorious, Technicolor, all-singing-all-dancing musical. We were living the dream. A dream in which we, the one third of the population under the age of 15, were the unwitting participants in a social experiment.

Though Cumbernauld was constructed from poured concrete and tarmac, there was an abundance of greenery in the town. We had playparks surrounded by swathes of grass and a wealth of shrub beds where dog roses grew into tangles worthy of Grimm. Shrubberies with less lethal foliage served as jungles where adventures could be had and dens were built while the transition from one neighbourhood to another was smudged by wooded glades. Bluebells grew in the spring and brambles in the autumn. The road system was designed with as much weight given to pedestrians as drivers, resulting in a complex pathway of bridges and underpasses. There were no traffic lights in Cumbernauld and there was not a single road that had to be crossed on foot. Thus, Cumbernauld became the safest town in Britain.

They built the town with children in mind, but the children they had in mind had skins of leather and bones of rubber. We never had to cross a road, but our play areas were as brutalist in design as the rest of the town. Some consisted of nothing more than concrete pipes set alongside boulders dug up in the building process. These boulder/pipe combos were scattered throughout town. When I was little, I couldn't pass one without crawling through the pipe, my enthusiasm fired by my one-time find of a five-pence piece lying half-buried in the sand coating the bottom of the pipe. Sand that wasn't sand but an accumulation of dank grit, stinking of piss. The stench was familiar, bringing to mind being crammed against adult legs in red telephone boxes, or picking at the paint on window frames while calls were made. It reminded me of the part of the toonie around the post office and the bookies where the air was made of grime.

The idea of a hard landscape making an ideal play area was expanded on when they built a playpark made entirely of concrete in Millcroft Road, near where we first lived in town. There was no greenery there. The only yielding surfaces were our bodies, but hundreds of kids lived in Millcroft Road and the concrete playpark was always thronging.

Many playparks in Cumbernauld were set in green places but the CDC (Cumbernauld Development Corporation) didn't want us growing up as a generation of grass-salved flimsies. To remedy the situation, they cut rectangles in the grass where the swings, roundabouts[10] and slides were to be sited and filled them with tarmac. Over time, the tarmac accumulated a patina of glass shards. In the 1970s, there was no such thing as soft play.

Our school playgrounds were coated in tarmac, our sports pitches surfaced with red blaes. We dangled and swung from metal monkey bars over gravel-strewn asphalt and made a game of snatching pebbles from beneath the spinning roundabouts. Skin was stripped, knuckles grazed, fingers scuffed.

When I was 9, I broke my left arm, snapping the ulna after falling in the school playground. I spent the afternoon at my desk as usual, not noticing anything wrong until the high school kids bashed into me on the way home and my arm wailed in protest. At home, when I peeled off my school blouse, my mother gasped at the sight of my arm all swollen like a boiled sausage. It was worth the pain for the ambulance ride to the Royal Infirmary in Glasgow. The driver put on the mee-maws to get through the traffic, then stopped on the way for a fish supper.

---

[10] Known in the US as a merry-go-round.

From the age of seven through 10, my knees were permanently scabbed. My dad tried to bribe me whole with money, but even a bribe of 50 pence was not enough to salve my knees. My scabs were a product of my environment.

But it wasn't all concrete. We were not starved of nature. From the end of our street, standing at the grassy bit, where the big tree grew up from the cobblestone castle, you could see the Campsie Hills with miles and miles of fields patchworked before them. There were woods and landscaped shrubberies so elaborate, little kids and even older boys or men could go on expeditions within them. It was on one such expedition that my pal and I found a soft porn magazine. We surveyed our find in complete silence, taking in the pouting lips, long hair, and bare breasts, but mostly we stared at the thick, dark triangles of pubic hair where the mystery lay.

Once the images had been scorched onto our retinas, we dropped the magazine where we had found it. My friend went to his granny's house for tea and I went home for mine. From then on, every time I was in the bushes, I kept my eye out for magazines filled with naked women, much in the same way that I crawled through concrete pipes looking for money.

Beyond the bushes, there were picnics at Fannyside Loch, treks through Red Fox Valley, and walks to Palacerigg Park Country Park where you'd get an acrid whiff of the resident red fox before seeing it run up and down, losing its mind in a wire cage. There were so many green spaces in town, that when my cousin from Govan came to visit, he thought the urban townscape of Cumbernauld was the countryside.

With its parks and playgrounds, schools and shops, footpaths and hedgerows, Cumbernauld was a utopia for families, but it was a utopia built in the brutalist style. The mean streets of Glasgow may have been abandoned for the town of tomorrow, but brutalism in 1970s Cumbernauld often strayed beyond architectural style. While the plumbing had changed for the better, old attitudes had been shipped in along with the population.

Chapter V. Do Not Play With Matches

Our new home in Cumbernauld was a three-bedroom council flat in an area called Carbrain. The flats were modern, built with clean lines, all rectangles and squares, a Legoland vision in greys and whites. The communal bins were located in big lockers at the bottom of our close[11] and each landing had a chute for rubbish. When you dropped in your waste, you could hear it tumble all the way to the bins below.

Back then, there was a lot of working-class pride in keeping your close clean. You didn't want to be a person with a dirty stair, and this extended to keeping the chute doors bright and shiny, but—no matter how polished they were—every time I opened one, there came that familiar whiff of something wet and rotten.

Outside the close was a communal drying area where one day I stood alongside another small child, both of us watching a big boy burning matches. *Not* playing with matches was ingrained into my psyche, along with not touching my dad's razor and not drinking out of the lemonade bottles under the kitchen sink.

It's not lemonade, Lorraine, my father told me. *It's cleaning fluid. You can't drink it. It's poison. It's not lemonade. Not lemonade. Not lemonade.*

In later years, I found out that the amber liquid was neither lemonade nor cleaning fluid, but whisky, siphoned from barrels on the merchant ships my father sailed on in the Hebrides. While he helped himself to his angel's share, my mother lived in fear of the excise man turning up at the door.

Don't play with matches. Don't play with matches. Don't play with matches.

The boy lit match after match, letting each one burn close to his fingers before dropping it and striking the next. I

---

[11] Close: Communal entry way, stairs and landings connecting the flats/apartments within a block of flats/tenement building.

was transfixed by the small flares and his boldness. Our silence, as with the later discovery of the porn mag in the bushes, intensified the illicit dalliance with the adult world of razor's edges, naked flames, pubic hair, and *not lemonade*.

I don't recall my first day at school. Either so traumatic that it has been wiped from my memory or, more likely, something I drifted through in my own little bubble. I was content in my bubble, lying in bed, looking at the faces created in the folds at the top of the curtains and seeing other worlds in a patch of moss. I imagined my toys coming alive at night and believed in witches and fairies, werewolves and vampires. I fantasised about living in a house underwater with sharks and whales and colourful fish swimming past my window and I thought that if I believed it strongly enough, I would be able to fly. My bubble was amazing but the problem with bubbles is that someone always comes along and bursts them.

My bubble survived my first couple years at school, more or less intact. Our teacher was firm but kindly. If you'd have asked me her age back then, I'd have put her at around 80. She couldn't have been that old, or anywhere like it, but at a time when our mothers wore mini-skirts, Mrs MacIntyre's pinafore and waved, set hair looked characteristic of a scratchy, old monochrome film.

She told us to be quiet but one day I was excited about something I'd made from Plasticine[12], I had an overwhelming urge to show it to the girl sitting beside me. I knew, absolutely knew, that I wasn't supposed to speak but I couldn't contain myself. I physically couldn't hold the words in and, as soon as they splurted from my mouth, Mrs MacIntyre sent me to stand in the corner of the classroom, facing the wall. As punishments went, I didn't mind it at all, and I positioned myself so that I could peek through the side of the curtain to look out the window. When I caught a glimpse of my mum pushing my baby sister in her pram, it was like seeing a secret.

---

[12] A brand of modelling clay, typically sold in bright colours. The name is now commonly used for any brand of children's clay, in the same way that clear sticky tapes are generally called Sellotape and most vacuum cleaners are known as Hoovers, no matter the manufacturer.

We were taught many things by Mrs MacIntyre. Though I was often distracted by events in my bubble, I quickly learned how to read. *Dick and Dora,* the pages read, *Nip the dog. Fluff the cat. Mummy and Daddy. Here is Dick with Dora. Dora runs to the tree.*

Cuisenaire rods were used to help us learn numbers. How smooth they felt and how ordered they were. Each rod, from the undyed 1cm cube, representing one, to the 10cm-long orange rod representing 10, had its own colour, and each had its own space in the box. We learned the words to "All Things Bright and Beautiful" and sang it at assembly, but the main thing we learned in those early years was how to queue.

When the bell rang in the morning, we queued in the playground, each class forming two lines, one of girls, one of boys. Access was denied until the lines were straight and silent and, only when we had been rendered sufficiently submissive, were we permitted to file into class. This operation was repeated throughout the day, after lunch and playtimes.

In the classroom, we queued for room-temperature milk, sipped through a straw from a pyramid-shaped carton. It tasted faintly of plastic and only just on the right side of turning. I grimaced as I sucked, miffed that I was always in the queue and never the milk monitor doling out waxy cartons from the crate. When we had craft projects to complete and needed help from the teacher, we spent more time queuing than doing. I even made my words queue in columns in my news jotter.

Monday	1	February
Today	we	must
not	play	near
the	fence	in
the	playground	because
it	is	being

painted.

We queued for tickets for school dinners then queued for the dinners twice over, once for something and potatoes then again for something and custard. We stood in long queues along long corridors, waiting for injections in our arms and sugar cubes that tasted the way the doctor's surgery smelled. The sugar contained a polio vaccination so that we wouldn't end up like the collection box statue of the sad little boy outside the chemist's shop.

We queued to get our heads inspected by the nit nurse. We queued for assembly, and we queued for gym. When we were in gym, we queued for equipment and sometimes we just queued, long lines of children walking up and down, weaving in and out of the spaces between, like synchronised swimmers. Always orderly, always keeping formation and thus obedience was turned into a game.

Chapter VI. Wee Maggie

After my dad left the merchant navy and got a job in a factory in Cumbernauld, he and my mum went on a night out and Wee Maggie—my father's mother—came out to babysit my sister and me. My dad left Wee Maggie with a quarter-bottle of whisky but, rather than slake her thirst, it piqued her appetite for more drink. When the quarter-bottle was done, she got me jacketed up, put my sister in her pram, and off we strolled to Bell's, the off-license near the train station. While I waited outside watching my sister, my granny went inside and got us both a sweetie, mine in a wrapper, hers in a bottle.

We went back home and, while I was in bed, my granny had a wee party to herself. When she was done partying, she took a notion to do my mother a favour by washing the living room curtains. I slept through the ensuing drama of my parents arriving home after a good night out to the sight of blankets in the window, dripping wet towels hanging over kitchen chairs, and my granny lying in a heap, snoring. My mother was mortified at the implication that her curtains needed washing and my granny never babysat for us again.

Billy Connolly once described the older women he saw in Glasgow as square coats with a pair of dangly legs hanging beneath. Wee Maggie was one such woman. Short and squishy as a Soreen Malt Loaf[13], she had false teeth and deep dimples. She was born in 1924 and her parents married three years later. They lived in Port Dundas, an industrial area to the north of Glasgow's city centre that once boasted the world's tallest chimney. My granny was eight when her father died of one kind of pneumonia, 11 when her mother remarried, and 14 when her mother died of another kind of pneumonia.

---

[13] A malt loaf is a type of sweet, chewy bread made with malt extract. It is sticky and usually sliced and spread with butter. Goes very well with a cup of tea. Soreen is to the malt loaf what Hoover is to vacuum cleaners.

Wee Maggie's step-father, John Markin, was a boot repairer by trade and signed the wedding certificate with an X. They lived for a time at 100 Cathedral Street, now the site of a bookshop for university students. By the time her mother died, they were living in the East End, not far from the Saracen's Head pub, known locally as the Sarrie Heid, above which my father would one day be born. Markin signed his wife's death certificate with his customary X and then he signed himself out of Maggie's life. By this time, age 15, Maggie had acquired an older boyfriend but, when she was in hospital being treated for rickets, the boyfriend took up with Maggie's big sister.

Rickets was a common affliction in Glasgow. The condition is caused by insufficient calcium and vitamin D, resulting in bones that are soft, weak, and painful. It can lead to deformities such as bowed legs and bowly legged men were a common sight when I was a kid. My father joked that they looked like cowboys who'd lost their horses. By 1940, Glasgow Corporation was trying to combat the condition by giving schoolchildren free cod liver oil and orange juice, but that was way too late to help my granny.

When Wee Maggie was due to be released by hospital, she didn't have an address and authorities wouldn't discharge her without one. Her sister eventually said she could use hers, though made it clear that that meant writing the address only. Maybe she worried Maggie would steal back the boyfriend.

Maggie was duly signed out of hospital but, at the age of 15, she was homeless and reduced to sleeping up closes. This is how she was living when she met my grandad. He was ten years older than Maggie and doing alright by himself on the black market, so much so that he was known as the Millionaire Jew. Though he was neither millionaire nor Jewish, he did at least have a decent coat on his back. He offered this coat to Maggie and, according to family legend, when she accepted it, he asked her if she wanted to marry him.

She accepted and they were wed in May 1940. She was 16, my grandad 25. Wee Maggie was by then working as a restaurant assistant and my grandad was a general labourer. By the time their first child was born in 1941, he was a gunner in the Royal Artillery.

Their first child was a daughter who died before she was a year old. In January 1942, Wee Maggie gave birth to her second child in a tenement flat above Sarrie Heid pub. The baby boy, who slept in a drawer, would one day become my father.

And so, before she turned 18, my granny had lost both parents, suffered painful ill-health, been made homeless, married, grieved the loss of a baby daughter, and given birth to a son. She went on to have two more children, both daughters. Though she was only 40 when I was born, the life she'd been allotted had etched its way deep into her face. She always looked old to me, as if it was impossible that she could ever have been young.

Chapter VII. This is the Modern World

It was a time of change. There was the old and the new. What went before and what came after. I was born into the era that came after and all that went before was lumped into the amorphous mass of my pre-existence. I knew the Second World War was real in the way I knew that Charles Dickens wrote *Oliver Twist* and that dinosaurs once walked the earth.

But the concept of time is abstract and even though both my parents were born in the early 1940s, WW2 seemed as distant to me as the Wild West or the Roman Empire. I wasn't aware that it was all around me, that the town I lived in had been created in response to the housing shortage created by Luftwaffe bombing campaigns, or that those same bombs were at least partly responsible for the wastelands in Glasgow, where grit rose in the gust and swirled like a litter-strewn Sahara sandstorm.

The war ended nineteen years before I was born but rationing went on until 1954 and the language of it never left my grandad. We called grocery shopping going for the messages, but my grandad always called it going for the rations: *Maggie's away oot fur the rations.*

I just went oot fur the rations.

To me, it was just another of his verbal quirks, like calling a poncho a poco. He never talked about the war or his experience of it, not to me and probably not to anyone.

My other grandad was a Canadian submariner from St John's, Newfoundland. He was killed by a German torpedo in the Battle of the Atlantic before my mother was born and before he could marry my grandmother. Having a child out of wedlock was severely frowned upon and so my mother became known as the wee bastard. Her entire life was overshadowed by the trauma of her early childhood. Though I didn't see it at the time, those same shadows crept around me. For a while at least, they were bleached out by the childhood sunshine of reading books, collecting tadpoles and playing in the dirt, but, all the while, they were there, stalking me.

My dad's father was 50 when I was born. I had friends whose fathers were around, or at least not far off, my grandad's age. They sat in their living rooms, staring at the television set in the corner. My dad wanted to be heard but these men were silent with storm clouds scudding through their veins and eyes that never strayed from the screen. I never knew if they genuinely couldn't see the young people in the same room as them or if it took all their will to ignore us.

They were old enough, some of them, to have served in the war. To have seen and perhaps done terrible things. Now they sat like stone statues watching the Fonz tease Mrs Cunningham. These fathers were from the past, of the same generation as the pinafore-wearing, set-haired teachers who taught us the achievements of Victorian men. They were from the time of imperial money. We were new, we were decimal.

The old imperial system of money had its roots in Ancient Rome, as illustrated by the abbreviation LSD, short for libra, solidus and denarius—Latin for pound, shilling and penny. Following the Norman Conquest in 1066, the pound was divided into 20 shillings, or 240 pennies, then in 1180, the coin system was reformed by Henry II and stayed that way until George Harrison was at number one with the hit "My Sweet Lord."

Decimal Day was a time of monumental shift in Britain. On the 15th of February 1971, the poetic language of the imperial system—crowns, florins, sixpences, farthings—was replaced with decimal new pence. Pennies were out, pence were in, 100 of them to the pound.

We were taught the decimal system at school, but, while decimal currency became compulsory, everything else in the real world was measured the old imperial way. At school, we were taught grams and kilograms, but we bought 2oz or a quarter (of a pound) of sweets from RS McColl's. Potatoes, sugar and flour were bought by the pound, shortened to lb, milk by the pint, and we ran for miles, not kilometres. We weighed ourselves in stones and pounds and measured our height in feet and inches, but, at school, it was centimetres and

metres, litres and kilometres. We were taught in the new way
while still living the old.

A quarter of a pound please of
chocolate peanuts, Liquorice Comfits,
Tom Thumb Pips, cherry lips,
pineapple chunks, chewing nuts,
fruit creams, jellybeans, sherbet straws,
aniseed balls, Jujubes, Kola Cubes,
chocolate raisins, coconut mushrooms,
dairy fudge, Soor plooms, lemon sherbets,
clove rock, sweet peanuts, acid drops,
Midget Gems, ginger creams, toffee whirls,
hard gums, crispets, Jazzies, Jelly Babies,
white mice, Snowy's
and two ounces please of
Army and Navy.

Chapter VIII.

New Home, New School, New Friends, New Games, New Rules.

Four months after the new money came in, we moved to the other side of the toonie. Our new home in Ravenswood was a three-bedroom council house with a garden. The houses were regimented in terraced rows on the side of a hill, all with the same grey slate roofs, white harled walls, single glazed windows, and the same breezeblock walls running in lines to mark the bottom of the gardens. Our house was on the end of the terrace beside the big steps. These were wide and shallow rather than big and had a dense shrubbery on either side. Jungles on my doorstep.

The houses had front porches, though rather than a box stuck onto the front, these were like boxes cut into the house, as though a final giant brick was missing from each one. The porches contained the bin locker and cellar, the doors of which faced the street while the front door was at right angles. The cellar stored bicycles and sledges and became a handy place to hide my jealousy when the other kids were eating pokey hats from the ice cream van and I wasn't allowed. One day my curiosity got the better of me and I turned the knob on the metal box attached to the cellar wall.

Sanitary Incinerator was printed on the front and the drawer on the bottom said **Empty Often**. When I turned the knob, the box ticked like a bomb about to go off and I ran away in a panic. It was years before I realised that it was a mini furnace for disposing of sanitary towels.

The front door opened onto the small middle landing where the telephone lived on its special table. The bathroom door faced the front door and beside it was the airing cupboard containing the gurgling water tank and my dad's scratchy Merchant Navy blanket. Seven stairs led up to the three bedrooms, two large enough to take a double bed and the other just big enough for a single bed. Seven stairs led down to the kitchen and living room. A few of the houses had the living room upstairs and two of three bedrooms downstairs, but everything else was uniform.

Our new garden was a miraculous place. We had grass all to ourselves. Our grass. Ours. It was overgrown when we moved in, hip-height to me. Long enough to roll around in, to get lost and have adventures. Emva Cream, whose real name was Allastair and I now called Uncle, came with a scythe and cut the grass. *Swish. Swish. Swish.*

New home, new school, new friends, new games, new rules to learn. Hidden rules, the kind that no-one ever told me about. The kind I was just supposed to know but never did.

The girls in my class told me they were playing at houses and that I could join in. They told me I could be the baby. I'd never played at houses, but I had a baby sister who cried a lot, so I squished up my face, closed my eyes and pretended to cry. When nothing happened, I opened my eyes and saw that I was on my own, that they'd all gone to play another game without me. It was the first inkling that I didn't fit in. That I didn't know how to be a girl.

Since the new school was about to break for the summer, they said I didn't have to start until next term but my parents thought it would be a good way for me to make friends for the summer holidays. Good theory. Didn't work.

As it turned out, my friend that summer long was a boy called Basher who lived just along the street, so not knowing girl games and girl rules didn't matter, for a time at least. Basher was a funny wee fellah with a pink, puckered face covered in freckles. He got his colouring from his mother who had big, blonde hair and was always done up in nice clothes and make-up. She was what we called back then a dolly bird. His dad was a big, old mountain of a man with black hair, shaved short so that it looked like his head was painted. He worked at the abattoir in Glasgow and, when we went to high school, he supplied one of the biology classes with bulls' eyes.

He put me in mind of Bluto from *Popeye* but, despite his terrifying appearance, he was nice man and I was really excited when he took Basher to the fete at Cumbernauld village in their orange VW camper van. When they got a dog, I went to their house and asked if I could take it for a walk. That was a thing back then. You could just rock up to someone's house and ask to take their dog out and mostly they said yes, but, on this occasion, Mr Basher turned me down: *You're too wee. The dog would be taking you for a walk.*

It was a Doberman pinscher and probably weighed the same as me, so he had a point.

On Saturday mornings, I'd stroll along to Basher's house to watch *H.R. Pufnstuf* on their colour telly. (Ours was still black-and-white and we only got two channels.) The star of the show was Jack Wild who was also the Artful Dodger in *Oliver!* My dad often took me to the pictures, sometimes with my cousin, and we'd been to see *Oliver!* I was bored at the bit when he cried about his mother. Fagin and the Artful Dodger were great, but the best bit was my dad letting me sit on the top of the double decker on the way home, something my mother never allowed because that's where the smokers sat.

Basher and I mostly palled around outside, playing in the bushes and just messing about. One memorable occasion, I stood watching him while he ate a Walnut Whip. In our house, Walnut Whips were the preserve of adults, and I was taken aback to see him eat one as casually as I would a Fizzy Lizzie. He pulled the walnut off and threw it aside, then bit off the chocolate at the top and began to lick out the fondant. As he nibbled his way down the chocolate sides, I was eaten up with jealousy.

I didn't think it could get any worse but then he finished the fondant and chucked away the thick, chocolate base. I was scandalised. Tossing the walnut aside was bad enough, but how could anyone throw away chocolate? As I stared at it lying in the gutter, I'm not going to deny it crossed my mind to pick it up. It was a bit gritty, a bit slabbery, but a good rinse under the cold tap and she'd be good to go. I'm still pleased that I didn't yield to my baser instincts.

That August, I turned seven and my mum laid out a dress for me to put on instead of my usual shorts and sloppy joe T-shirt. The sun was shining and I could see Basher playing outside his house, so I took a wander along.

Why are you all dressed up? he asked. His tone implied that I must have some pretty big ideas about myself.

It's my birthday.

I expected him to wish me a happy birthday. Instead, he grunted and went back to whatever it was he was doing with those two bits of stone.

Deflated, I turned around and walked home, and every step of the way, I hated the stupid sandals I had to wear with the stupid dress.

It's the first birthday of mine that I can remember and the only thing I remember about it is Basher bursting my bubble.

Chapter IX.  British Bulldog

When I went back to school after the summer, there were 42 of us in the class. There weren't enough classrooms in the school, so we were taught in a cavernous, gloomy room beside the gym while they built huts for us in the playground. The teacher was a nice woman who didn't shout at the boy who shit himself in class and she didn't shout at me when I spewed in the middle of a class project about Robert Peel.

The teachers were obsessed with us doing projects about Victorian men who had done something or other. In two years, I'd be taken on a school trip to David Livingstone's house in Blantyre. He was one of those missionary-types who went to Africa to tell people they were wrong about everything and then got himself lost. He's mostly famous for being found by an explorer called Stanley who is supposed to have said, *Dr Livingstone, I presume?* His house was about the most boring thing a 9-year-old could ever visit and, as it pished down with rain all afternoon, we weren't allowed to play rounders in the park afterwards and had to eat our packed lunches on the bus on the way home.

Robert Peel didn't go to Africa. He invented policemen who were called bobbies and peelers after his name, which is everything you need to know about Robert Peel and, if they'd stopped it there, it would have been fine, but the project went on and on and on until I was bored to my core. I couldn't stand it. I didn't want to write or draw or listen to another thing to do with this dreary man and his worthy life.

Why did they always have to teach us this tiresome, tedious stuff? Why couldn't they teach us about interesting things like dinosaurs and sharks and jungles filled with man-eating plants and quicksand that swallowed you up—instead of these wearisome men who all looked like they had a stick jammed up their arse.

I thought that I was only pretending to feel sick when I put my hand up, that I was sick of the project, not actually sick in myself. The teacher sent me to sit at the bench at the side of the class and told me to put my head down. Its smooth surface felt cool and soothing against my hot cheeks. And then I opened my mouth and puked up the world. Wave after wave of vomit flowed across the counter and cascaded onto the floor. A short while later, I puked up again. This time at home, over the orange nylon cushion covers on the settee. I was sent to bed and bought a bottle of Lucozade.

Before it was reinvented as a sports drink, Lucozade was sold as a sort of medicine—*Lucozade aids recovery*. It had a metallic taste and the bottle was wrapped in crinkly, orange cellophane. The whole point of being ill was that you were allowed to drink Lucozade.

When we moved into our classroom in the huts, everything was bright and airy and smelled of new. My new teacher wore twin sets and pearls and her dark hair was styled like Elizabeth Taylor's in the 1950s. She wore rings, many, many rings. It was in this class that I learned that England was bigger than Scotland. The other kids laughed at me for not knowing this already, but I couldn't get my head around how anything could be bigger than where I was, as it seemed so enormous. I learned about Robert the Bruce and the try, try and try again spider story. The story stuck because of the spider but was told in isolation and I had no idea who this Robert the Bruce was other than he wasn't Victorian.

The teacher with the Elizabeth Taylor hairdo told us to be quiet. She told us several times over and, finally, the class settled down but I had words bursting like Opal Fruits in my mouth and I had to say them. I couldn't resist. They were too good to keep to myself, but, when I tried to share, nobody wanted them. The teacher was getting angrier and my classmates told me to shush, but I kept talking. I couldn't help it. I talked and I didn't stop until the teacher called me to her desk and smacked me in front of the class. I didn't care that she hit me, that was normal. It was the rings. If it wasn't for all those rings, it wouldn't have hurt at all.

At break, we mostly played in our own groups, but, occasionally, a mass of kids joined together. Sometimes, the game was in looking for a game. It began with three or four boys swaggering across the tarmac, arms linked, chanting, *Who wants a game of Cow-boys and Ind-i-ans?* A long straggly line was created as more and more kids linked on, all of us chanting, *Who wants a game of Cow-boys and Ind-i-ans? Who wants a game of Cow-boys and Ind-i-ans?* This went on until the bell rang and we lined up for class without ever playing Cowboys and Indians.

No chanting was required when we came together to play British Bulldog. Suddenly, acting with a hive mind, we knew it was happening. We flooded down to the red blaes pitch and gathered along one length. On the opposite side, a lone boy—one of the older kids—faced us. The air crackled with anticipation and then up went the cry, *British Bulldog, British Bulldog, 1, 2, 3.*

We charged and the boy ran out to meet us, tagging as many as he could before we got to the other side. Everyone he tagged joined him and, as we ran back and forth, his side grew in number and became harder to dodge. There came a point when it was almost a relief to be caught. Then I could hunt instead of being chased. It was an exhilarating game to play, especially for someone like me, who didn't understand the rules of most sports. All you had to do was run as fast as you could from A to B without being caught. There was extreme joy in running in a pack. You could feel the excitement in yourself and all around and no-one was judging, no-one commenting, because in that moment we were all part of it.

Once you'd been tagged, all you had to do was face the diminishing charging horde and tag as many other people as you could. We picked them off one by one, grabbing them by their school jumpers or the crooks of their elbows until the few survivors were converged upon. As we crowded in, some of the smaller ones fell and were trampled in the stampede. Finally, only one runner remained. He, and it was almost always a boy, was the winner.

Injuries were sustained, tears shed, complaints made, and then British Bulldog was banned along with Space Dust, clackers, running with pencils, Tom Thumb Pips and the game where kids made themselves black out. This involved hunching down with your arms wrapped around your knees and holding your breath until you keeled over. The playground was filled with all these kids looking like little mushrooms. I never partook in this game, as I was scared of blacking out and never coming back in. Despite the British Bulldog ban, there were spontaneous outbreaks of the game and we'd get a few charges in before Mr Duthie, the janny, turned up.

Mr Duthie lived in the special janitor's house at the end of the pitch. It was a neat house with a tidy garden and looked too small for Mr Duthie, who was a bear of a man with a grizzled beard. In the winter months, he wore a Russian-style fur hat. This being Scotland, it was mostly winter and so he was mostly wearing his hat.

One day, he saw me playing on the grass instead of the tarmac playground and wrote my name down in his little, black book. I spent the next few days in a state of trepidation, waiting for the call to the headie's office, which would spiral into trouble at home, and all for running on a bit of grass, but the call never came. It seemed that Mr Duthie had played a fine joke on me. All the same, he was not a man to be trifled with and the sight of him bearing down on our illicit game of British Bulldog sent us scattering like crisp pokes on a breeze.

Chapter X.

Children Are Starving in Africa

Tea was a drink and the name of our evening meal. We ate ours at the yellow Formica table in the kitchen. For most of my childhood, this was not a meal I looked forward to, as, at that time in Scotland, it was thought that a child would die for the lack of a potato. The only exception was in the summer when a salad without potatoes was permitted, although there was always the danger that my mother would open a tin of Heinz Potato Salad and slub a spoonful onto my plate.

Potatoes came in three varieties: mash, roast and boiled. At school dinners, mashed potatoes were dished out in scoops like ice-cream and sat on the plate in a neat ball. At home, they came in a thick scud. For many years, I wondered why roast potatoes were called roast potatoes, for, in our house, they were peeled then par boiled before being deep fried in the chip pan. Why, I wondered, were they not called fried potatoes? But questioning the norm was not encouraged and usually led to ridicule so I kept my mouth shut.

The worst of all potatoes was the boiled old potato. These were peeled before boiling and sat large, dead and dry on the plate, as tempting a morsel as a box of chalk.

A cousin to the potato was the chip. There was great excitement in the school dinner queue when chips were served but always, by the time I got to the hatch, there were none left and two balls of mash were thudded onto my plate instead. Not that I was keen on chips, not at all—at least not home-made chips, as they were only smaller versions of my mum's roast potatoes, their saving grace being that they contained less potato—but I eventually learned to love chip shop chips when I discovered that they were very soft and didn't taste of potato but only of the half pint of malt vinegar and dredging of salt I poured over them.

The only comfort when my mum served us roast potatoes was that they had crispy skins I could scratch my fork at and nibble on. If I dissected them enough, it would finally look as though I had eaten some of the content. Mash I could manage if it was scooped up a tiny bit at a time with a forkful of mince (mince and tatties were known as Govan caviar), but with the large, plain boiled potato, there was nowhere to hide, and the daunting sight of them piled on my plate filled me with dread.

Mum, I don't like potatoes.
Be quiet and eat your potatoes.
But I don't like them.
Everyone likes potatoes.
I don't.
EAT YOUR POTATOES!

This last from my dad, his voice as shocking as a fist thumping on the table. His tone was not to be argued with and so I sat and picked at my potatoes with my fork, trying to worry them into non-existence.

At school dinners, I developed two techniques for potato avoidance. Instead of eating the potatoes, I carefully packed them into the sides of my mouth, like a hamster but without the benefit of cheek pouches, and then asked for permission to go to the toilet. I must have sounded like Marlon Brando in *The Godfather*, but that film was yet to be made and no eyebrow was raised as I was sent on my way. Locked safely in the toilet cubicle, I scooped out the potato and flushed it away. My idea wasn't too far removed from the method used to dump-tunnel earth in *The Great Escape*. It's a pity there were no pockets in my school pinafore, as I could have stuffed them with potatoes for later disposal in the playground.

As time went on, the drawbacks of the potato-in-cheek method became clear. No matter how careful I was cramming them into my cheeks, I inevitably ended up with potato taste and texture on my tongue and, as time went on, I became less tolerant of the fragments. I began gagging when scooping them out and, when gagging turned to retching, I knew I had to find another way. The answer lay in physics. Years later, I wrote a noir crime novel called *Boyle's Law*. Boyle's Law is also a law of physics which states that when pressure doubles, volume halves. Without realising I was testing this law, I exerted extreme fork pressure on my school dinner mash and succeeded in reducing the volume sufficiently to hide it under a slime of boiled cabbage or beneath a skin of congealed gravy, so it looked as though I had eaten most of my dinner.

Unfortunately, the same trick wouldn't suffice at home. I tried the potato-in-cheek method, but there were only so many times I could be excused from the table without arousing suspicion. Besides which, gagging and retching were more of a problem at home, as the walls were thin and my parent's ears were attuned to mischief. Neither was Boyle's Law an option at home. At school dinners, adults roamed the alleys between tables, scanning for children not eating properly. To miss the sweep of their gaze, all I had to do was get the timing right, a bit like dodging the searchlights in *The Great Escape*. At home, there was always at least one parent at the table watching, always watching. A new tactic was required.

I ate slowly. Very, very slowly. I cut tiny pieces of whatever meat was on my plate and held it in my mouth for a long time before beginning the process of chewing. Finally, when everyone else had eaten and all the plates had been cleared but mine, they went to the living room to watch television, leaving me in splendid isolation in the kitchen.

In all likelihood, I only had to eat at a moderate pace at home, for we ate as though stoking the fire of an engine. There was little in the way of talk at the table. Wine and conversation had not yet been invented, at least not in our house. Eating was a function rather than a pleasure, especially when my dad was in a bad mood. All that mattered at the time was that I was able to drag it out long enough to be left alone to dispose of the potatoes at my leisure.

The first time I carried out my plan, I sat at the table and looked around, thinking where to put them. The bin would not do, for my mother would surely spot them there. Though only early evening, this being during the ten months of winter, it was already dark outside and I thought of spitting them out the window, but the sun would at some point rise and my mother would surely query why there was a mound of mashed potato on the back doorstep. I was smart enough to realise that it was no use wishing for a stray cat to come along and eat them, nor was there any sense in trying to hide them in a cupboard or drawer in my mother's domain. She was bound to discover them almost immediately. I was on the brink of tears and exhaustion when, finally, the solution came to me.

I stared into the dark plug hole at the bottom of the kitchen sink, thinking it was so obvious and perfect a place to dispose of potatoes, I wondered why I had not thought of it. I began pressing the potatoes into the hole, jabbing them through the strainer, very pleased with my smart thinking as I ran the tap to rinse away the bits. Soon, my plate was empty.

I went through to the living room to watch television.

Did you eat all your dinner?

Yes, Dad.

I gave my reply happy in the knowledge that I had left no evidence.

Slow eating became a habit and each night I disposed of my potatoes down the sink. I kept this up for as long as it takes to block a kitchen pipe. When my dad removed the U-bend and four stone of mashed potatoes fell out, my parents had an epiphany.

You really don't like potatoes, do you, Lorraine?

There was no use in saying I'd been trying to tell them that for years. Besides, it very much looked as though I wasn't in big trouble. No mention had been made of my dad's belt called Rastus and he wasn't giving me one of his looks. In fact, my parents seemed amused. I wasn't going to risk ruining the moment and so I simply replied, *No, I don't like potatoes.*

At school, I continued doubling the pressure and halving the volume, but, from that day on, I did not have to eat potatoes at home.

I had sensory issues with other foods, but none as bad as with potatoes for the simple reason that no other food was as ubiquitous. Beyond food, there were fabrics I couldn't bear to touch and, as these were mainly synthetic, it wasn't too handy a trait to have, but in the 1970s nobody knew about sensory issues. Anything that deviated from the norm was not tolerated and I was labeled fussy, picky, annoying, weird.

It wasn't just potatoes that made school dinners Hell. Custard was compulsory and, on the rare days that custard was not served, rice pudding or semolina were compulsory instead. It was a trinity sent forth from Hell, but custard, with its almost daily appearance and cloying smell, so thick I could taste it even out in the corridor, was by far the worst.

We had no autonomy. Not only was self-expression not encouraged, it was actively discouraged. You were not allowed to not like things. *There are children starving in Africa.* And so I stood in line, collecting my cake from the hatch then moving along to the inevitability of the giant pot.

Can I have just a small amount please?

If the dinner lady was nice, she'd take pity on me and dribble only a small amount of custard into my bowl. If I was very lucky, the custard would barely touch the cake and I'd be able to eat most of my flies' graveyard or coconut sponge. Caramel shortbread, with its almost transparent layer of gooey spread on a thin, biscuit base with a few chocolate sprinkles on top, was my favourite, but with it being so shallow, it didn't take much custard to ruin the experience.

If the dinner lady thought I was cheeky for asking— *Why are you so ungrateful?* was the implication—a small lagoon of custard pooled around my cake. In this situation, I could eat my way through the top and leave the contaminated edges. From small lagoon, it went straight to End of Days. I was polite, always polite. I was too well-conditioned to be anything else, but every time I stood in line, I was fearful of what was going to happen to my cake. The worst of the dinner ladies could smell my fear and it excited them, the excitement triggering a sense of power that compelled them to slop an apocalyptic amount of custard into my bowl, covering my cake entirely. They'd see my wee crestfallen face and smirk at me, satisfied with their unholy work. *Don't you know there are children starving in Africa?* they seemed to say.

When it finally became too much to cope with, I told my mother and she wrote a note asking the dinner ladies not to give me custard. The next day I was so excited to go to the dinner hall. I would finally have my cake and eat it, but when I handed the note over, the dinner lady looked at me as though I'd just pissed in her soup.

I'll let you off today, but, from now on, if you don't want custard, you'll need a doctor's note.

There was no way my mother was taking me to the doctor for a note about custard and so, for one day only, I ate my cake unsullied. Every day after was a battle of wills, but no matter how much they tried to force it on me, I did not, would not, eat custard.

Not then. Not ever.

Chapter XI.

Dirt

One of the most popular toys in the 1970s was dirt. Dirt had two main advantages over other playthings. First, it was free. Second, you didn't have to wait until your birthday or Christmas hoping to get some, only to be forced to mask your disappointment because your parents had bought you a nice new vest instead of a Girls World styling head. All you had to do was go out and find some, which wasn't hard, as dirt was everywhere and came in a range of types. The fun to be had depended on the type you found. I had the best of times sitting on the kerb, scraping at gutter dirt with a stick. There was a great sense of satisfaction in prising it out then studying the dank space left behind. On lucky days, I'd see something small, white and terrifying writhing as it sought to flee the light.

A brilliant sledging hill was lost to the children of Cumbernauld when construction began on a colossal new tax office. The upside was that the works unleashed a cracking array of dirt. During the build period, a huge wedge of land was gouged out of the hill, creating a valley to be traversed on the way to school. We had to go down one embankment then cross the rutted, muddy road that was the entrance to the building site before going back up the other side.

There was a little hut beside the newly created road where a one-armed man kept watch. The man had a weather-beaten face and dark, curling hair and wore his empty sleeve pinned to the front of his jacket. I stopped to talk to him on my way to and from school, taking the opportunity to peer into his shed where a transistor radio, a newspaper, and a tub of sandwiches sat on a narrow, wooden shelf.

There were many puddles and much mud on this new route to school and I discovered that if I dipped my fingers in a certain type of light grey mud, it dried quickly, tightening as it did so before cracking and flaking off, leaving my fingers surprisingly clean and nice and soft. I didn't realise I was giving my fingers the equivalent of a face mask. I can't recall how many random puddles and pools of mud I stuck my hands into before discovering the magical qualities of grey clay, but, once I knew about it, I couldn't pass a patch without getting stuck in. The call was irresistible. Even when I was with my mum, the pleasure was worth the telling off.

Many hundreds of tons of earth were shifted as the ground was prepared for construction, and a large mound of it was dumped at the bottom of the tax office hill, near where a boy called Robert lived. For a few weeks, we were best friends and we claimed the mound as our own. We sat on top of it, chipping away at the earth with stones, ambitious to chip it away to nothing. We grunted in satisfaction, giving a running commentary as we prised away clods and rooted out stones.

That was a good one.

Yeah, really good.

Look at this big bit.

That's really good.

We congratulated ourselves on doing a great job as we tossed the clumps into the undergrowth below.

We're helping the men, we said to each other, clarted in muck and dust, and as happy as two little kids could be.

Another great thing to play with was expanded polystyrene. Ripe was my jealousy when someone got their hands on a chunk and sauntered along the street, scraping it against harled walls, releasing thousands of perfect pearls of white polymer in their wake. Big boys did it casually, as though unaware of the envious glances cast their way. A talented scraper could release such a quantity of beads that it was possible to snatch them from the air or harvest them from my clothing and squish them between my fingers.

On the rare occasions that I was the one scraping the polystyrene, my joy was deep. I'd watch the beads riding the breeze before skittering into the gutter. From the gutter, they'd be washed into the drains and make their way to the sea, where they would plug the blowhole of a sperm whale or clog the throat of a baby dolphin, but I was blissfully unaware of such impacts. Synthetic materials like polystyrene and plastic were everywhere. Synthetic was now. Synthetic was us.

We wore it, we made furniture out of it, we even decorated with it.

My love of polystyrene went beyond delighting in the cascades of beads liberated by scraping it against a harled wall. I loved its use in packaging and imagined tribes of little people and strange animals living within the white, geometric landscapes. I loved the squidgy, semi-resistant feel of it, how you could gouge it and compress it and cut it, how it was tough yet malleable. The squeak when two pieces rubbed together sent a shiver through my teeth.

If I saw it, I wanted to touch it.

My father was not a man overly endowed with DIY skills. While fixing a hook to the back of the bathroom door, he used a screw longer than the depth of the door and was surprised when it broke through the other side. Maybe he thought it would disappear into a fourth dimension. The hole was a source of endless annoyance to my mother, but my dad wasn't minded to do anything about it until he came home from the pub one night and had an overwhelming urge to remedy the situation. It would be, he thought, a lovely surprise for my mum in the morning. And indeed, she was surprised when she saw that the door had been patched with a piece of tape that had been painted over in a shade of brown several times darker than the rest of the door.

Despite his lack of prowess in decorating, my dad undertook tiling the bathroom ceiling. Expanded polystyrene is inflammable, so it probably wasn't the best choice to cover a ceiling, but, this being the 1970s, there was scant regard for self-preservation and the bathroom might as well be as flammable as the rest of the house.

The polystyrene tiles were a source of fascination for me. When I was on the toilet, I'd stare up at them with longing and I'd gaze at them as I washed my hands, ignoring the crick in my neck as I battled the urge to touch.

In the following days and weeks, my parents were confounded by the small dents mysteriously appearing in a patch of ceiling above the sink. It hadn't occurred to them that I would climb from the toilet to the sink, then onto the narrow shelf behind the sink and brace my back to the wall, head turned against the slope of the ceiling to enjoy prodding my finger into the polystyrene.

I didn't go daft; I only made a few holes at a time and only when the urge outweighed the risk of the climbing and balancing and getting caught. It didn't occur to me that my activities had been noted until my parents discussed it in front of me. They were genuinely perplexed, wondering what kind of weirdness had befallen their ceiling. I blushed a guilty shade of scarlet and confessed.

They were scarcely less baffled when I told them what I'd been doing and so my punishment was limited to a lecture about how I could have broken my neck, my back, the sink, the toilet, and told not to do it again. The tiles were replaced and I was forced to resist the urge to sink my fingers into the lovely squeaky, squidgy whiteness.

But at least there was always dirt.

Chapter XII. The Bee Game

There were many grassy bits, but only one was called the Grassy Bit. This was at the end of my street where the big tree rose from a cobble castle. It was where I rolled down the hill, over and over then stood up and staggered, giddy and giggling. It was where we had grass fights after the men had been 'round cutting the grass, leaving it in big, tempting piles. I'd get into trouble later for going home with my clothes covered in green stains but, the next time the men cut the grass, I'd do it over again.

There was a swathe of grass a couple rows up from us, where nobody ever played because it was full of shit produced by a big, black dog called Toby. There was no dog shit at the Grassy Bit but there were bees. It was common practice to capture a bee and keep it as a pet in a cleaned jam jar with holes punctured in the lid so that it could breathe. Adding a couple dog roses created a wonderful environment for your pet bee.

Soaking dog rose petals in water for a few days made a lovely perfume. On one occasion, I kept my concoction in a jar behind my bedroom curtains. After a couple days, my mother remarked on the smell, complaining that next door's cat must have got in and peed in my room. When she discovered the jar, she made me pour my lovely perfume away.

In the summer of 1972, the entrance to a bee nest was discovered on the slope at the Grassy Bit and a new game was invented. A horde of us gathered in an excited semi-circle, watching as a big boy covered the hole with a jam jar. Within seconds, the jar filled with bees. At first, they had space to move around and you could see them banging against the glass, but all the time more and more bees were cramming inside and soon the jar was vibrating with a mass of insects. They kept on coming and when there were so many bees inside that he could hold on no longer, he let it go and sprang back. For a moment, we watched the jar roll down the grassy bank, spewing out bees, but when they spiralled into the air, we screamed and ran away, laughing and terrified at the same time. After a while, when all the bees had flown away, we drifted back to the Grassy Bit and did it all over again.

No-one got stung, not until the day Basher borrowed my bike and used it to cycle along to the Grassy Bit. I was sitting on my porch, waiting for him to come back, when he came howling and crying and hollering along the street, his face a deep shade of pink. It was against the law of the land for boys to cry and so I watched with interest as he ran past my house, tears spraying from his eyes. I realised he'd been stung and, following on from that realization, came another. Basher had left my bike at the Grassy Bit.

Never had my street seemed as long as it did on that day when I went to retrieve my bike. My heart was thudding and there was a tremble in my legs as I listened hard for the slightest hint of buzzing in the air. Finally, I reached the Grassy Bit and there, laying abandoned on the grass, was my red bike. I stared at it for a while, listening and watching for bees and then slowly, slowly I approached. Heart still pounding, I picked it up then cycled like the wind until I got home.

I heard Basher had been stung in the eye and, when I saw him, there was a pink lump on the lower rim of his eye that wasn't there before. The lump never went away and Basher never talked to me again. He ignored me when I said hello and, after a while, I stopped trying. We were friends and then we weren't. I never knew why. Perhaps it was because I saw him crying or maybe he associated me with the pain of being stung in the eye. It had been my bike he'd been on after all. My red bike, and we all knew that red made bees angry.

I had no guilt watching the bees being riled up in that way and nobody else said a thing about it either. Bees weren't considered the good guys back then, in fact, they were thought mad, bad and dangerous to know. A reputation underlined throughout the decade with horror stories in the news about the threat of hybrid bees invading the USA and the slew of bee-fear films including *Killer Bees, The Savage Bees* and big-bucks disaster movie *The Swarm* with Michael Caine heading up a starry ensemble cast.

After the summer of the bee game, I began my fourth year at primary school and that October we celebrated the 50th birthday of Uncle Allastair. His birthday was on the 4th of October, a date he made sure I'd never forget. On long walks to Palacerigg Country Park, he encouraged me to sing, *Remember, remember, the 4th of October*, in the same sing-song rhythm as *Remember, remember, the 5th of November, gunpowder, treason and plot.*[14]

By this time, he and his wife, Margo, had comfortably inveigled their way into our family. They came to our house for evenings of drinking and laughter. Margo drank Martini[15] and lemonade and, when I kissed her goodnight, the bristles on her chin stabbed me in the face. Each November, they bought an advent calendar for my sister and me. A small thing, but, by the creation of such traditions, they became part of the fabric of our lives.

They also altered the fabric of our life, as before them, meals out were a rare treat confined to the celebration we had on Fair Friday. The Glasgow Fair was a traditional holiday, usually the last two weeks in July, when all the shops and factories closed, shutting early on Fair Friday. The train stations were stowed out on Fair Saturday as thousands of people left the city to go *doon the watter* to the Firth of Clyde or the Ayrshire coast and nobody had heard of anybody who went abroad for their holidays. The tradition was carried on in Cumbernauld and, after my dad's factory closed on Fair Friday,

---

[14] "Gunpowder, treason and plot" is a line from a nursery rhyme referring to the Gunpowder Plot of 1605 when Guy Fawkes, along with a group of fellow Catholics, conspired to assassinate the Protestant King James I (James VI of Scotland) and replace him with a Catholic monarch. The failed attempt is celebrated on 5 November and known as Guy Fawkes Night. Typically, an effigy called a Guy is burnt on a bonfire to the accompaniment of fireworks. In Scotland, Guy Fawkes Night is often called Bonfire Night, a celebration that pre-dates the Gunpowder Plot and is related to the ancient Celtic festival of Samhain.

[15] A brand name for a type of vermouth.

it became our tradition to go out for a meal to the local Reo Stakis restaurant.

Reo Stakis was a Cypriot man who settled in Glasgow and, in the 1960s, established a chain of restaurants that were affordable enough for the working-class to treat themselves to a nice meal out. Going to the Stakis was a big deal in our house. My sister and I had a glass of orange juice for starters, the glass sitting on a paper doily, while my mum had soup and a bread roll and my dad had prawn cocktail. My parents didn't believe in undercooking anything and would order their steaks well-done, fillet for my mum, T-bone for my dad, while we would either have fish and chips or gammon steaks served with a pineapple ring and a maraschino cherry in the middle. There was ice cream for afters but the best part was that we were allowed a glass of Coca-Cola. This was served with a straw and cocktail stick spearing a slice of orange and maraschino cherry. It was the kind of drink that made a little kid feel pretty grown-up. The MacDougs were of course there, but, when we went out on the 4th of October in 1972, it was all about him—Uncle Allastair.

We went to the Abetone for his birthday, a restaurant at the top of the toonie—the same place that owned the chippy. My mother was an excellent baker and baked him a huge square cake covered with blue-icing sugar rosettes and 50 candles, which we brought to the restaurant. After our meal, the staff lit the candles and brought the cake out and everyone sang "Happy Birthday."

He lapped up the attention, his white hair slicked back as it always was, snake eyes hidden by the glint of candles reflected in his glasses while his lips, narrow, wet and pink, smiled at his surrogate family before pursing and blowing.

Chapter XIII.  The Wee Bastard

Shandus was a baby when they killed him, about three feet long from snout to tail. Bold, black taxidermy stitches criss-crossed his belly and, when I peered into his gaping mouth, I could see yellow stuffing clogging his throat. It was a thrill to run my fingers over his sharp crocodile teeth and I liked to fantasise that he came alive at night when no-one was watching. I tested this theory by placing a Rowntree's Fruit Pastille on his tongue. The next time I was at Gran and Grandad Brannigan's, I couldn't wait to see if he'd eaten it and was disappointed to find it still there. Shandus the baby crocodile was well and truly dead.

My mother's parents lived on the top floor on a block of flats in Eccles Street, Springburn, so high up, you had to switch lifts to get right to the top. Although their building was only four miles from where my father's parents lived in Carntyne, the two homes were worlds apart. In Carntyne, life was stark. My grandad gave me bookies' slips to draw on to amuse myself, but, at Eccles Street, there was a wealth of exotic distractions. I always asked Gran Brannigan to switch on her fountain and she always obliged. This was a three-tier affair with plastic lily pads in the bottom pool. It lit up when she switched it on and water trickled from one tier to the next. As far as I was concerned, it was a thing of beauty, like something out of a Disney film.

As well as a stuffed crocodile and a plastic fountain, there were cigarette cards, fancy cocktail stirrers, and Flamenco dancer dolls in long, frilly dresses to play with. When we visited on New Year's Day, my sister and I were given ginger cordial to drink. It was supposed to be diluted but we were served it in small, gold-rimmed glasses straight from the bottle. Thick and sweet, the cordial caught our throats and burned in a delicious way as it went down. Jenny Brannigan was a small, neat, stylish woman and, like my mother, she had dark brown hair. When I called her Granny she told me, *I'm too young to be a granny—call me Grandmama*. Grandmama didn't sound any younger to me than granny. I thought she was kidding and decided to call her Gran. Edwin Brannigan was a tall man with silvered hair and a strong, handsome face. He looked like a cross between Stewart Granger and Jeff Chandler. They seemed different to us and different animals altogether from my other granny and grandad. There was a black-and-white photograph of them snapped by a street photographer as they strolled along some foreign street, her in a snug dress and peep-toe sandals, him in a sharp suit, a cigarette between his fingers. They looked like movie stars.

They were the only people I knew who went on foreign holidays and sometimes they brought me back a present. My favourite was an oversized black pencil that had a plastic shrunken head on the end with long, black hair growing out of the skull. I kept it in my special drawer with the rest of my treasures—Bazooka Joe wrappers, Smartie lids, skipping rope, marbles, bits of Lego—and took it out occasionally to examine the grim lines etched deep into the grimacing face. I loved that shrunken head.

They were visiting us in Cumbernauld when she gave it to me and I took her upstairs to show off the bedroom I shared with my sister, the walls of which were covered in posters, mostly from *Jackie* magazine. I had a couple of special giant posters. These came as magazines that opened out so that the words were on one side and the poster on the other. I was excited when my dad brought an Osmond one home for me. Though slightly deflated that he'd chosen Jimmy rather than Donny, I read every word and memorised Jimmy's big hit, "Long-Haired Lover from Liverpool," then stuck his larger-than-life-size face on the wall over my bed.

My cousin, who always had more discerning musical taste, gave me a right slagging for it, which put me in the position of defending the artistic integrity of Little Jimmy Osmond. I also had a giant pull-out poster of the other major musical child star of the day, Michael Jackson, and it was this my grandmother chose to comment on: *I don't like darkies.*

Killed the mood stone dead.

Despite Shandus, the fountain, and all the other wonders within my grandmother's flat, my favourite place to be when we visited them was out on their veranda where I stood for ages, looking at the other blocks of flats and the tiny houses beyond and the cars moving on the roads and the railway tracks and the big, green rectangle of the football park, and further yet, the great haze of the city hanging like a painted backdrop, and always, always, always I'd be fighting the urge to climb up and launch myself off the side. I could picture myself doing it, and I could feel the rush of air as I swooped between the high-rises with the birds. But despite the urge and the longing, I knew I couldn't fly and my fantasy wasn't the only illusion in Eccles Street.

The man I called Grandad wasn't my grandad and there was no window behind the frilly curtains and blind in their bathroom. The curtains hid a blank wall and I'd be well into my teenage years before my mother finally told me that Brannigan wasn't her father. I'd always wondered why they had different names but broaching such subjects only led to a drop in temperature and tightened mouths. When they finally came, the words were brittle.

My grandmother Jenny was 22 and pregnant with my mother when her husband-to-be was killed in action. He died when his submarine was torpedoed by a German U-boat during the Battle of the Atlantic. He was from St John's, Newfoundland. His family knew about Jenny and that she was pregnant. They kept in touch for several years, sending over clothes and chocolate, which Jenny hoarded for herself.

Within two years of my mother being born, Jenny met another man. Edwin Brannigan was a 28-year-old seaman in the Royal Navy and a bootmaker by trade. He called my mother The Wee Bastard and, after he and Jenny were married in December 1944, The Wee Bastard was put out to be brought up by Jenny's widowed mother, who in later years became known as Old Maw. My mother and Old Maw lived in Milton Street in Cowcaddens, pronounced *Coo-caddens*, an area just north of Glasgow city centre that includes the Theatre Royal and Cineworld (formerly the site of Green's Playhouse and the Glasgow Apollo). In the 18th century, Cowcaddens was a village beyond the city where cows were pastured. Just as Springburn was indelibly altered with the coming of the railway, Cowcaddens was forever changed when the Forth and Clyde Canal opened in 1790. Industrial development began in the form of mills and foundries, granaries and warehouses, and housing soon followed. It was absorbed by the city in 1846 and, by the end of the century, degenerated to slum conditions.

My mother and Old Maw lived in a single end with an outside toilet. Old Maw cooked on a range in the fireplace and one of my mother's favourite treats was saps, this being bread soaked in warm milk and sprinkled with sugar. They shared a bed in the recess and, on Sunday evenings, they'd go to the Mission Hall and belt out classics such as "Yield Not to Temptation" and "Onward Christian Soldiers". After the singing and preaching, there was tea and an iced bun for my mum. She played in the streets, having more dray-pulling Clydesdale horses on them than cars, and, when the police wagon came along and loaded drunks into the back, she and her pals ran along behind it, chanting, *The Black Mar-i-a, the Black Mar-i-a*[16].

During her childhood, she contracted cutaneous diphtheria, an incredibly painful disease that left her with pockmarks on her body. In the meantime, her mother had borne two children to Edwin Brannigan: Samantha in 1947 and Eddie in 1949. My mother was never included in family photographs and was bitter that her siblings were taken to the dentist while she was not.

After leaving school at 15, she went to work behind the counter at Peacock's bakery. She met my father there when he came in to buy empire biscuits. He asked her out and they went dancing at the Dennistoun Palais. She was 16, he 17. They were married within a year. Though he was shy back then, my father was a charmer and Old Maw, who farted as she walked, loved him and called him Long Legs.

---

[16] A term for a police vehicle originating from a Bostonian woman in 1820 renowned for aiding cops in sorting out unruly prisoners.

Though Old Maw adored him, relations with the rest of my mother's family were not so smooth. From a young age, I had the notion that my dad didn't like Grandad Brannigan. He always referred to him as Brannigan, never by his first name and always with a sneer implied. Although I perceived the edge, it still came as a shock to find out the truth. The hurt was in the lie, and it was made worse by being kept up for so long, but, in our house, knowledge was the preserve of my parents and pain was my mother's domain.

Mind your business.

What have you got to cry about?

You don't know how lucky you are.

When the Brannigans came to spend Christmas Day with us, I still didn't know that the man I called Grandad wasn't. My dad went to Eccles Street to pick them up before the MacDougs arrived but they weren't at ours for long before my grandad was horizontal in front of the electric fire.

Mum, Grandad's on the floor.

Mum, what's wrong with Grandad?

My sister and I were hustled out of the way, and then,

Your grandad's not well. He has to go home.

It was a grey day, the kind that made the street look like a black-and-white photograph. I was standing on the pavement when my father drove them away, Grandad slumped in the back, Gran staring out of the window on my side, her eyes gazing into nowhere. I waved at her as they went by, but she didn't look at me. I don't think she even saw me. It was as though I wasn't there at all.

I was given the impression that my grandad's heart was the problem and then nobody said anything. It was years before I understood that it was nothing to do with his heart but that he'd been absolutely mortal drunk. It was hardly the first time something like that had happened in the family, but perhaps it was the excuse my mother or father or both needed to cut ties. Whatever else went on, I was told nothing. It was as though the Brannigans had ceased to exist. After that Christmas Day, I never saw them, or Shandus, again.

Chapter XIV.  Brown

There was only one colour in the 1970s and that colour was brown. The carpets were brown, the wallpaper was brown, the furniture was brown, and when they weren't black and white, the television programmes were brown. Even my flared trousers that melted when I stood too close to the electric fire were brown. It was as though a cup of Camp's ersatz coffee had been poured over our nicotine-stained world.

In the 1970s, everybody smoked everywhere and, if you were too young to have learned to appreciate smoking first-hand, you could buy cigarettes for the responsible adult in your life to enjoy the benefits of secondary smoking in your own home. My father often sent me to the corner shop to buy him a half ounce of Golden Virginia tobacco. Off I'd trot in my slippers, money in hand, with maybe a little extra to get myself something from the penny tray that sat at the edge of the counter, where everyone could cough and sneeze and rub their grubby fingers over the MB Bars and Penny Dainties and Parma Violets and white chocolate mice and Flying Saucers and Fruit Salad and Black Jacks with casually racist wrappers and Lucky Tatties and giant Gobstoppers.

The shop assistants—not even the scary lady who always regarded me with a downturned mouth and pinprick eyes—thought nothing of handing the tobacco, all wrapped up in smart green and gold packaging, to eight-year-old me. There were no age restrictions on buying it—or, if there were, none that anyone paid attention to because smoking was the norm.

On single-deck buses, smokers sat at the back. In double-deckers, they got the whole of the upstairs. The ceilings and walls of pubs were stained nicotine yellow. People smoked in restaurants, and cafes, stubbing their fags out in yolks of half-eaten fried eggs or drowning them in their dregs of tea.

At the pictures, there was the main film plus the support film and sometimes a cartoon along with adverts and trailers shown in a continuous loop. If you missed the start of the film, you stayed in your seat until it came on again and finally the film made sense. All through the sitting and watching and catching up, you could see the swirl of exhaled smoke in the projector's beam. Every film I watched, from *Bambi* and *Sleeping Beauty* to *King Kong vs. Mecha Kong*, was watched through a blue cigarette haze.

At school, our teacher tasked us with designing posters illustrating the hazards of smoking. One boy drew a grave with a headstone that looked like a cigarette. I was wildly jealous that I hadn't thought of it, but someone said he'd ripped it off and everyone slagged him off and that soothed my green eyes. After we made our posters, the teacher emerged from the thick cigarette fug in the staffroom and told us to go home and tell our parents that smoking was bad.

My grandad's fingers were stained yellow from years of smoking Capstan full strength, these made of pure tar. My granny smoked Embassy Regal and so did Great Auntie Joanie. She held her cigarettes in a mysteriously birdlike manner: between fingers cruelly twisted and crippled with arthritis. After years of making roll-ups from Golden Virginia, my father switched to tailor-made, sending me out to buy golden boxes of Benson & Hedges.

My mother gave up smoking before I was born but, at Christmas, she'd take me to the tobacco shop near George Square in Glasgow so that I could buy a present for my dad. The bus into Glasgow took us past the Wills's Whiffs cigarette factory on Alexandra Parade. At its height, it produced 260 million cigarettes a week. For anyone who over-imbibed, it was conveniently located beside the sprawl of the Royal Infirmary, which was conveniently located beside the Necropolis. Glasgow's City of the Dead.

In the tobacco shop, I'd buy slim panatelas in a plastic tube printed to look like Santa Claus, or, if I'd saved up enough pocket money, a five-pack of fat King Edward cigars. On Christmas Day, my father amused me by blowing perfect smoke circles at the living room ceiling before tapping the ash into the cut-glass ashtray.

As news leaked out that smoking gave you cancer, people tried dissuading children by telling us that it wasn't big, it wasn't clever, and it wasn't cool. While all the cool kids were smoking, I was sniffing my dad's old tobacco tins.

Not being cool enough to smoke cigarettes, I ate them instead. Candy cigarettes were white with pink tips so you could pretend they were lit. They came in cardboard cartons with cartoon characters like Tom and Jerry and Popeye on the front. I pretended I was smoking by holding them between my fingers and blowing out imaginary wisps of blue haze. I puffed on the stems of liquorice pipes and teased out single strands of Spanish Gold sweet coconut tobacco from a pack folded like Golden Virginia. But, of all the tobacco confectionery, chocolate cigarettes were the best. These came in soft cartons like Camels and were wrapped in edible paper as thin as Rizla rolling papers. I pretend-smoked them, feeling sophisticated as I imagined myself a character in one of the melodramas I enjoyed watching on TV. Bette Davis in *Now, Voyager* or Joan Crawford in *Mildred Pierce*.

Those who actually smoked and developed a 20-to-40-a-day habit, didn't have time between puffs for eating sweetie cigarettes. They didn't have time for eating anything. That's the real reason hardly anyone was fat in the 1970s. They were all too busy smoking.

Lucky them, for this was the decade when processed food boomed. One of the most popular TV adverts showed Martian robots mocking humans for going to the trouble of peeling and boiling potatoes when they could open a packet of Cadbury's Smash instead. While potatoes came dehydrated in packets, cheese could be squeezed from a tube, instant curries rattled in boxes and, Smedley's sausage rolls, pale and raw, were packed six to a tin. It was surely more pleasant by far to have your palate numbed by nicotine than to be familiar with the full, unadulterated taste of a Spam fritter.

My mother would sooner have died than make mashed potatoes from a packet or buy a box of crispy pancakes, but food in the 1970s was generally pretty awful and—even in our potato-peeling, pastry-rolling house—processed food rocked. I loved Smedley's tinned sausage rolls. Mince rounds, which were mostly pastry and hardly any mince, were a treat and my sister and I were wild for a tiny, mousse-like portion of Angel Delight whisked up and served in a Pyrex sundae glass.

By process of elimination, my favourite dinner was salad. No potatoes, no cooked vegetables, and no danger of stew making an appearance on the plate. Exotic ingredients like peppers, cherry tomatoes and iceberg lettuce hadn't been invented and salad dressing was unheard of. Olive oil was only bought in tiny bottles from a chemist to be warmed up to cure earache. A person had to be insane to drizzle earache cure on their salad. Your basic salad consisted of a few leaves of round lettuce (limp, tasting vaguely of grass), three slices of cucumber and two quarter-wedges of tomato. For ham salad, you'd add a couple slices of ham. For corned beef salad—well, you get the picture. My favourite was cheese salad, which included a wee pile of grated cheddar. Almost all cheese was cheddar and all cheddar was orange.

Occasionally, my mother went wild and bought a hard wedge of Edam, which was even blander than the mild cheddar but came with the excitement factor of a red-wax skin I could peel off. Salads were fancied up with the addition of hard-boiled eggs, a bit of grated carrot, a couple spring onions (we called them syboes) and a sprinkling of cress, and if I was lucky there was a pickled onion. If you'd asked for something that seems quite ordinary today, say hummus, you'd have been asked in turn if you were feeling okay.

The only other meal I looked forward to was ham ribs. These were boiled in the big pot and the stock used to make lentil soup. My mother did most of the cooking, but my dad cooked a fry up at the weekends and occasionally turned his hand to a pan of soup. When my mother was in hospital, he decided to make the one pan last all week. What began as lentil became Scotch broth and then swamp water. There were tears at the table when he served up that treat.

Processed food didn't relate to anything in the real world. I mean there was nothing about a Smedley's tinned sausage roll that made you think it had once been alive, but when it was ribs for dinner, you knew exactly what you were eating. Each of us got a sheet on our plate that looked as though it had been cleaved from the pig 10 minutes ago. There was no finessing this meal. We tore the ribs apart with our hands, our cheeks becoming sticky as we gnawed and chewed the salty meat. We sucked and scraped until every scrap of pink flesh had been stripped away and then, in a scene worthy of Sawney Bean[17], the long, white bones were stacked high in a bowl in the middle of the table.

If we were lucky, there was Angel Delight to follow. Butterscotch flavour, of course, because—like everything else in the 1970s—butterscotch was brown.

---

[17] According to Scottish folklore, in the 16th century, Sawney Bean and his 45-strong clan lived in a cave on the Ayrshire Coast. Over the course of 25 years, they were said to be responsible for murdering and cannibalising over 1,000 people. Historians cite lack of evidence and no-one knows for sure whether there is any truth in the legend.

Chapter XV.

Teacher, Leave That Kid Alone

I hated going to the toilet at school. Instead of proper toilet paper, squares of Izal were dispensed from cardboard boxes. Izal looked like cheap, shiny tracing paper and had none of the properties you'd expect from toilet paper. It wasn't absorbent. It smeared rather than wiped and it was hard. If unlucky, you could end up with a shredded arse. Washing your hands with a pink brick of carbolic soap wasn't any more comforting. It stripped off the top layer of skin, leaving your hands reeking of antiseptic for hours, so, even if your arse hadn't been properly wiped, at least you smelled clean. Uncomfortable though they were, Izal and carbolic were nothing compared to the ultimate horror of school toilets. They were an echo chamber.

Not only could everyone hear you doing your business, the sound of every bit of that business was amplified. A cloak of shame and embarrassment shrouded bodily functions. The tiniest puff of a fart elicited a mass outbreak of sniggering from outwith the cubicle while, behind the snibbed door, my face was burning brighter and pinker than the carbolic. A mass of Izal thrown down the pan helped deaden the tell-tale tinkle of pee hitting water. Farts and tinkles were bad enough, but Hell mend you if you ever made a plopping sound. I got through 13 years of school without once going for a shit there.

One trick to bypass the embarrassment was to flush the toilet and pee at the same time. The drawback was that you then had to wait for the cistern to refill to get rid of the toilet paper. No way did you want someone coming in behind you and seeing that. Time is indeed relative. Two minutes waiting for a school cistern to refill was an agony, especially when the Boss Girl began chanting, *I can see your feet, I can see your feet*, followed by demands to know what you were doing in there. Frenemy was a word waiting to happen.

My philosophy was to avoid the school toilets except in times of extreme duress. This was made easier by the fact we weren't encouraged to drink water or any other hydrating liquids. After Maggie milk-snatcher Thatcher stopped free school milk in 1971, it was possible to go through an entire day of lessons, lunch, playtime and gym class without drinking anything at all. Pee ranging in colour from dandelion yellow to Irn-Bru[18] orange was considered normal, but, despite the desiccation of my internal organs, I was occasionally obliged to make use of the school facilities.

I'd just turned eight when I joined Mrs Gilp's class. A narrow woman with a tight face framed by rigidly styled dark hair, she fixed us with her hooded eyes and laid down the law. Allowing pupils to go to the toilet during lessons was one of the many things she did not tolerate in her classroom. She was one of those teachers who thought any kid needing to go to the bathroom was *UP TO NO GOOD*. Those who tested her by putting up a hand to ask received a withering look and a scolding. Permission was always denied.

One day, when the class was working quietly, my body betrayed me. I needed to go to the toilet but was too frightened to ask permission. I didn't want her shouting at me and I really didn't want everyone staring while she did her shouting. Soon the urge was too great to deny, but what to do? I couldn't risk humiliation by asking and I couldn't just sit there at my desk and pee. So, I came up with a plan. I went to the work box on the counter at the side of the classroom and pretended to look through it while I stood with my legs apart and relieved myself on the floor. Simple yet effective.

The deed done, I returned to my desk, pants wet, bladder empty, and got on with my work. It wasn't long before Mrs Gilp spotted the puddle on the floor.

---

[18] Irn-Bru, known as Scotland's *other* national drink (as opposed to whisky), is the country's best-selling soda. The taste has mellowed since, but, back in the 1970s, it seemed to grab you by the back of the throat. It is frequently used as a hangover cure.

Who did this?

Everyone looked at each other but no-one spoke.

Who did this? she asked again.

Again, her demand was met with silence. If anyone had spotted me in the act, no-one was telling, least of all myself. Usually quick to blush, I didn't even go red in the face. Fear had drained the blushing from me, and self-preservation kept me silent even in the face of growing tension.

After several more demands to know *who did this*, she seemed to give up and we all went back to our work. But she wasn't done yet. Mrs Gilp had an ace up her sleeve. When the bell rang for break, she announced that, as it was a lovely day, we could leave our coats in the cloakroom. She'd never concerned herself with whether we froze or roasted in the playground but of course everyone left off their coats and I had no choice but to do the same. I knew she was going to nab me as soon as she saw the damp patch on my skirt, but I was helpless to prevent it and the inevitability only heightened the horror of it happening. She made no secret of hauling me out of line and I could hear the whispers all around me.

That's her.

That's the one who peed on the classroom floor.

Once she'd made sure everyone knew who the culprit was, Mrs Gilp marched me to a special room where used pants were kept for wetters. I had to peel off my sodden pants and put on an old grey pair that some other kid—or *kids*—had been wearing. Then she had a go at me: *Why did you do that? Why didn't you ask to go to the toilet?*

The reasons were clear in my mind, but the words were as tangled in my mouth as seaweed on the strandline. How could I possibly explain to this woman that it was because I was scared of her that I couldn't ask?

I was sent home to get changed out of my skirt. I couldn't take the humiliation of being pointed at and laughed at and called Pissy Pants as I walked past the playground. So I tied my jacket around my waist to cover the wet patch and went the long way home.

Mrs Gilp was mean, but she wasn't the worst. That award belonged to Mrs Stark. Mrs Gilp withered with her tongue look but Mrs Stark beat you into submission. There were teachers who never used the belt, but Mrs Stark thrived on it. One day in her class after she told us to be quiet, a boy's pencil rolled off his desk. I liked this boy. He was a bit daft but he was never mean. All the same, he was one of those boys always in trouble. It was like the teachers were allergic to him.

I sat right beside him and it was dead obvious the thundering of his pencil and the mighty thud of it hitting the floor was not an act of provocation, but Mrs Stark was a teacher who belted children for the nothingest of reasons.

She called him to her desk to receive his punishment. He flopped out of his seat, all arms and legs and walked to the front of the class, the tense sway in his shoulders managing to convey resignation, frustration and fear. He was one of her favourite victims and knew the drill well. Without being asked, he put out his hands, one on top of the other, palm up, the stacking of hands making it harder to pull away. Mrs Stark drew back the thick, leather belt and struck him across the hand. She struck him again, three times on each hand. I flinched at every one of those six lashes. We all did.

The boy refused to give in to tears as he was belted but, as he returned to his desk, I could see them smarting his eyes as readily as I could see the raw, red weals rising across his hands and wrists. After a moment, he hunched over, hands clasped in front of his face so nobody could see he was crying.

That should never have been normal.

Chapter XVI.

Daily Bread

Aside from a nod to the baby Jesus at Christmas and watching *Ben-Hur* on the telly at Easter, the only manifestation of religion in our home was my mother's vague belief in a vague version of a Christian god coupled with her solid disapproval of taking the Lord's name in vain. When I was a wee girl, she taught me to kneel by my bed every night and say my prayers. *God bless Mummy, God bless Daddy, God bless my baby sister, God bless Granny, God bless Grandad...* and on it went to include whatever random people I'd seen that day.

She instilled in me a sense of God's presence, that He was all around us, watching over us all the time. I interpreted this invisible presence as an intrusion. I didn't want to be watched all the time, especially not when I was on the toilet. While she believed in God, she didn't believe in going to mass. My first experience of going to church was when my pal and I took ourselves of a Sunday morning after being told by another kid that they gave you free sweeties. We blagged our way into Kildrum Sunday School and, after hearing a few stories about Jesus and singing "Jesus Wants Me For A Sunbeam", we were rewarded with a single Smartie each and told not to come back without our parents.

My father was brought up a Catholic, but he never bought into it. *I was a child, what did I have to confess?* When the nuns at school heard him swearing, they threatened to wash his mouth out with carbolic. He wasn't standing for that, so he ran out of the classroom, yelling, *Fuck the Pope.* He never went back to that school and loathed the church forever after.

At primary school, we said the Lord's Prayer every day, but the meaning of the words was never explained and every time we said the bit about *give us this day our daily bread*, I pictured a Mothers Pride plain loaf.

When we first moved to Ravenswood, our next-door neighbours were a family from Stornoway, who spoke Gaelic at home and went to the Free Church. My dad had friends in Stornoway from his time in the Merchant Navy and one of these was a man called George. I thought my luck was in when my mother put aside her knitting needles for a Singer sewing machine powered by foot treadle. Finally, no more enforced wearing of the loopy, woollen hats she knitted that buttoned under my chin. Then George gave my dad a bolt of Harris tweed from which my mother used her sewing machine to stitch me a pair of trousers I was forced to wear. Within two days, my thighs were chafed raw.

There were no offerings of tweed from our new neighbours, but I did have my first slice of Arctic Roll in their house and my first game of Scrabble. They had three children, the eldest of whom was a girl who had the bad luck to be a couple years older than me so was often lumbered with my company on her mother's orders. This included taking me along to the Campaigners, a military-style youth group run by the Free Church. Sort of like the Brownies, but with lots of standing to attention and a lot more God. The Free Church was in Carbrain and the Carbrain kids loved the Campaigners so much, they'd clamber up to the church hall windows and bang on the glass while we were Campaigning away in our blue shirts, berets and neckerchiefs.

Each session began with some Christian soldiering.

Fall in, eyes to the front, shoulders back.

A-TEN-SHUN!

Wheel left, wheel right, stand easy.

I've always had a bit of a problem telling my left from my right so, at best, I was a beat behind and, occasionally, I'd be facing the wrong way altogether.

One of the skills I learned at Campaigners along with how to stand easy and to *A-TEN-SHUN* was how to set a table. I don't know if they gave badges out the way the Brownies did, but, if they did, I never got one. It wasn't a complicated table setting. One placemat, one knife, one fork, and two spoons for soup and pudding. When the Commander-in-Chief came to inspect mine, she said it would be very good if a left-handed person was coming to dinner.

Left wheel, right wheel, stand easy.

One night they treated us to a talk about leprosy and showed us slides of people hanging in bits. Duly terrorised, we were given plastic tubes to take home. Each tube could hold 20 five-pence coins and we were under orders to fill them for the lepers. It made a change from feeling guilty about the starving children in Africa.

Near the end of every session, we sat cross-legged on the floor and were read a story from the Bible. I can only remember the one about the Good Samaritan so maybe they read us the same story every week. One evening when we were all sitting on the floor, waiting to hear the story, the Commander-in-Chief said, *We've noticed that some of you aren't going to church.*

Oh no, they were talking about me! My head frizzled.

Now, I want you to raise your hand if you haven't been going to church.

My first thought was to simply not put up my hand. But then I was sure to be caught out in a lie, so up it went. The situation grew worse because now they were asking everyone with their hand up *why* they hadn't been going. My mind went into panic-fuelled overdrive.

Why didn't I go to church? I had no idea. I just didn't, but I couldn't say that. But what could I say? Who could I blame? Usually, I could come up with something but, on this occasion with them working through the other non-goers towards me, I had nothing but a complete blank. It was horrible, but then it was my turn and a miracle happened.

It's okay, Lorraine, you can put your hand down. We know you go to St Mungo's.

I was off the hook. Better still, I was off the hook on a lie that I didn't have to tell, for not only did I not go to the Free Church, I also did not go to St Mungo's. But I was taken there by the school at Christmas and Easter so I could nod and agree yes, I did go to St Mungo's. It was a lie, but also not a lie.

Amen.

Chapter XVII.  **Car**

Though the town of Cumbernauld was new, there had been settlements on the site since ancient times. The Antonine Wall was built by the Romans to mark the most northerly frontier of their empire. Three metres high and five meters wide, it spanned the width of Scotland from the River Clyde on the west to the Forth on the east. 2,000 years later, its remains could still be seen in Cumbernauld, whose name comes from the Gaelic *Comar nan Allt*, meaning *the meeting of the waters*. Poetic though it sounds, the waters of Cumbernauld—Luggie Water and Red Burn—don't meet.

With plenty of smaller burns as well as the Forth & Clyde Canal and Fannyside Loch close by, Cumbernauld had an abundance of fresh water, but the town was a long way from the coast and I was besotted by the sea. My first crush was Marine Boy, a cartoon character in a Saturday morning TV show. My mum's PK Chewing Gum looked like the oxy-gum Marine Boy used to breathe underwater and, when I managed to wheedle a piece out of her, I fantasised I was joining Marine Boy on his underwater adventures for the Ocean Patrol. For more sea-related excitement, there was nothing I loved better than to snuggle up to my dad and get him to tell stories from the Merchant Navy.

My favourite was about using joints of meat snaffled from the galley to feed sharks from the side of the ship at night. He and his mates used spotlights to watch the sharks thresh about the Red Sea as they tore at raw meat. Another good one was about him swimming in the open ocean when something touched his leg. He swam like Hell's fury to the ship without looking back, barely touching the ladder as he scrambled aboard. Only then, from the safety of the deck, did he see the distinctive bladders of the venomous Portuguese man o' war drifting on the water, long, stinging tentacles trailing behind itself.

Picnics at Fannyside Loch and paddling in the Luggie river were all very well, but I yearned for the excitement of the sea. My dad yearned to win the pools and every Saturday, when the football results came on the telly, we all had to shush while he checked his coupon.

Motherwell 2 - Airdrieonians 0.

Partick Thistle 0 - Rangers 1.

Albion Rovers 2 - Hamilton Academical 2.

Alloa Athletic 4 - Stenhousemuir 1...

One week in 1973, his roar rattled the windows when his coupon finally came up. He won just over 300 pounds. Even then that wasn't a life-changing amount—at least not in a mansion-buying, gold-plated taps, fancy car kind of way, but it was enough to alter ours.

The year before, we'd gone on our biggest summer holiday to the Isle of Man. Our first family holiday was cancelled when I caught chicken pox the day before Fair Friday. The following year, we went on holiday by train down the Ayrshire Coast to Saltcoats, a grey place by the sea. We stayed in a tenement flat and took the daughter of a family friend with us. She was a year or so older than me and we shared the bed in the recess. She wet the bed one night and, because I was the youngest and she didn't own up, I got the blame. My dad got really mad because he thought I was telling lies so he put me over his knee, pulled down my pants and thrashed me with his open hand. I screamed and cried, *Don't, Daddy, please no, I didn't do it.*

See, when you're a little kid and the responsible adult tells you that hitting you hurts them more than it hurts you? They're lying. It hurt like a bastard. After I'd been leathered, the other girl decided to own up and then it was all guilt and sorries and justifications and that's all there is to be said about Saltcoats.

The next time we went on holiday, we took a train to Ardrossan and boarded a ship that took us across the Irish Sea to the Isle of Man. We stayed in a guesthouse in Douglas, the four of us in two double-beds in one room. The landlady gave us vast swamps of bubbling-hot Irish stew for dinner on boiling-hot days and, every evening when she cleared the table, she commented on the food I hadn't eaten and called me fussy and my mum and dad laughed while I stared at the table.

My parents loved the Isle of Man, so after my dad won the pools, we went back but stayed in a hotel. My mum and dad had a room with a sea view and my sister and I shared one that looked over the back alley. We had money. We could do things. My dad took me pony trekking and deep-sea fishing while my mum and sister went for cream teas. Then all four of us went to a wax museum. There was a special section that had waxworks of Nazis stomping ankle-deep in someone's chest, Nazis whipping someone else with barbed wire, and Nazis pulling out people's fingernails with pliers. I paid close attention so that when I went back to school, I could tell my friends in great detail about all I had seen.

We posted Manx kippers to my grandad and went to a magical place called Summerland, which was full of waterfalls and tropical plants and birds flying about. It had bars and restaurants, live shows, and a funfair downstairs. My dad bought the man in charge of the funfair a few pints so the man kept an eye on my sister and me while we rode the rides for free all night and my mum and dad sat upstairs, watching the show. Summerland was the best place ever.

A few days after we went home, I was watching TV with my cousin and Summerland came on the news. It had gone on fire. Lots of people were dead and others were injured and the building engulfed by flames. Summerland was gone forever.

There was the holiday, but the main impact of winning the pools was that my dad could afford to buy a car from the scrappy. With the blue Ford Escort came freedom to roam, to explore, to visit the coast. When my dad was on early shift during the summer holidays, he'd come home at 1 pm, collect my sister and me to go to Glasgow, pick up my grandad and sometimes my granny then head down to Maidens on the Ayrshire Coast. My grandad made no concession to being at the seaside and dotted over the rocks and sand in his heavy, black coat.

My dad taught me how to go rock-pooling. We'd scramble around, looking for a rock that could be flipped over or rolled onto its side then watch as all the creatures living below scrambled for cover. And he showed me how to pick up crabs without getting nipped. I collected heaps of them in a red plastic bucket shaped like a castle. My grandad howled with laughter when one managed to sink its claw into the fleshy pad on the tip of my index finger and refused to let go. While I screamed and hopped around like a character from *The Beano*[19], he pointed at me, tears of laughter streaming down his face.

When I wasn't destroying ecosystems, I'd stand in the water, staring out at the horizon, imagining a huge waterfall where the ocean fell over the end of the earth. This is what I was doing when I saw a school of basking sharks swimming not far from shore. It was one thing knowing in theory that sharks swam in our waters, *seeing* them was something different. To me, sharks were almost fantasy creatures, as foreign, mysterious and exciting as jungles, volcanoes and quicksand, and now here I was, standing at the edge of a Scottish beach, the familiar cold of the water nipping at my legs as I watched the triangular fins cruise up and down.

Our car didn't just cruise up the coast. It meant more we saw more of my granny and grandad at their home in Carntyne. They lived in a second-floor tenement flat that always smelled of gas from the boiler in the scullery. From the heavy, wooden doors to the coal bunker in the hall, the fabric of the place was solid and industrial, a nod to the area's coal-mining past. On the way there, we'd pass a rock-face with **Trust in the Lord** painted in white, Gothic script and I'd always look out for the stark chimneys of Barlinnie Prison.

Boys sometimes lobbed half-bricks at us as we drove up the hill to where my grandparents lived in Myreside Place and, when we got there, we had to take turns sitting at the window, watching to make sure no-one stole the tyres or tried to set fire to our motor.

---

[19] A popular weekly comic published in Dundee, Scotland, by DC Thomson, featuring such iconic characters as Dennis the Menace and his dog Gnasher, the Bash Street Kids and Minnie the Minx.

They'd lived there since my dad was at school, moving from their tenement in Weir Street, Govan, without telling him. When he went home to the empty house, it was a neighbour who told him his family moved to Carntyne, some eight miles away at the eastern extremity of the city. One of my favourite things was when my dad pointed at the scar on the back of the living room door from when my granny threw a poker at him when he was a boy. He ran out, slamming the door behind him, and the poker clattered into it instead of him. I thought it was funny but my granny was never pleased at the telling of the story, scowling and muttering that he'd been giving her cheek.

They had a coal fire in the living room and there was a time I watched my grandad light the fire then hold a sheet of newspaper across the fireplace. I grew up with an electric fire so knew nothing of creating a draught to encourage flames. I thought he was mental. I was even more excited when he let the newspaper go and the suck of the fire kept it in place. He went to the scullery and had only been gone a moment when the paper burst into flames. I watched it burn, thinking this must be the intention but, when my grandad came back, he had a go at me.

Heavens' sake—Why didn't you tell me it was burning?

I was upset and confused. Upset because he was my grandad and my grandad never gave me into trouble. Confused because what did he expect to happen if he held a sheet of paper in front of an open fire? I couldn't find the words to articulate my thoughts and so I gawped at him, feeling miffed because he thought I was stupid.

The floor was covered in a patchwork of worn lino while on the ceiling wires looped across the room to the light fittings. One night, when my granny had been at the whisky, one of the wires caught her gaze and niggled at her until she was muttering under her breath about the *effing wire*. The sight of it incensed her until she could stand it no more, so she fetched a chair and a pair of scissors and cut the offending wire in two. The electric shock blew her across the room and shorted the house.

I quite often got a biscuit at my granny's. An Orange Club if I was really lucky, otherwise a Garibaldi or a fig roll. On rare occasions, there was a paper bag from the baker filled with snowballs—sponge cake sandwiched with raspberry jam and coated in coconut.

Granny and Granddad had a lodger called Jimmy Green. I tried to play a trick on Jimmy by offering him a hot sweets I'd bought at Tam Shepherds Trick Shop. They were supposed to set your mouth on fire, but the joke backfired on me when he asked for another. Jimmy's tastebuds were blown from a lifetime of whisky and cigarettes and the hot sweet was the first thing he'd tasted in years. I gifted him the whole bag.

Before visiting my grandparents, we sometimes went to the Barras, a mix of shops and pubs, street stalls and market halls, in the East End of Glasgow. The name derived from the handcarts, or barrows/barras, the old hawkers used. The street traders were known for their patter crowds gathered to. They sold anything from ham ribs to curtains to toys, their spiel delivered at full throttle and with plenty of jokes, often at the expense of someone in the audience. You didn't just go to the Barras to look for a bargain. You went for the experience and one of the experiences was the Loch Fyne, a wee café on London Road. The window was piled high with cooked whelks[20] (winkles). These were scooped up to order, rattled into a paper bag with the top folded over and secured with a pin you used to eat the whelks.

Inside, the tables were crushed together and the air was steamy, smelling as though someone had just brought a big pan of sea water to the boil, which wasn't far from the truth. The Loch Fyne had a limited menu. If you didn't like mussels or whelks, there wasn't going to be much there to please you. My mother didn't like either and couldn't stand the smell of the place, so it was always just my dad and me.

They have a chewy texture with a salty tang and look like something you might sneeze out if you have a particularly

---

[20] Whelk is a general term for a sea snail. In some parts of Scotland, whelk specifically refers to a type of small, edible sea snail w/ an inky blue shell. In many other places, these are known as winkles (short for the species periwinkle). Whelks are very common on the west seashore, where they can be picked from rocks at low tide.

bad cold. Although I had all sorts of sensory issues going on with food texture—e.g. potatoes, custard, rice pudding—this did not apply to seafood. The bones in herring fish never bothered me. We ate it with brown bread and butter to wash down the bones, and I'd happily eat crabs, whelks, and cockles.

I also loved mussels until I was poisoned by them one time too many. This after my dad had the genius idea of picking them from a harbour wall when the tide was low. Mussels filter water and are good at cleaning it, so we were dining on mussels that had absorbed all the waste from the harbour. My mother was raging at my dad for poisoning me and he had to look after me while I puked myself inside out. Couldn't eat mussels after that.

But this was before then, so we'd order a plate of mussels each, orange and plump, eaten with the fingers. There was nothing fancy going on, no messing with the moules, but there was a bottle of malt vinegar on the table if you fancied a splash. Dad occasionally treated himself to a clappy doo. This was an especially large mussel and not something I was inclined to eat. It was too much mussel for me, the lips and frills and other strange bits too obvious to ignore. Sometimes, he'd wash his meal down with a mug of mussel brae. This was the grey liquid from the boiling pot. These days, you could maybe get away with calling it a juice or some such, but you'd need a good stretch of the imagination. I tried it once and got a mouthful of grit. Once we had our fill, my dad ordered a few bags of whelks for Granny, Grandad and Jimmy to eat in front of the fire.

The car also meant trips to Kelvingrove Art Gallery and Museum, where I looked for a long time at the model of the Tyrannosaurus rex with its sharp teeth and tiny arms, and to the Transport Museum where they let you sit on an old tram like the ones my mum and dad used to ride on. One Sunday when my dad was bored, we went on a run to Glasgow Airport to watch the planes take off and land. At that time, you could just wander in and sit in a big viewing lounge upstairs. The four of us went on a day trip to the Trossachs—Rob Roy country. In Callander, we walked along the riverside and had lunch at a Chinese restaurant, this a big treat. My mum, my sister and I all thought the chicken and sweetcorn soup tasted funny and didn't eat it. My dad didn't want to waste the money, so he ate the whole lot and the next day his arse exploded in the toilets at Calderpark Zoo.

When we first moved to Cumbernauld, hardly anyone we knew had a car but, by the time we got one, car ownership was fairly normal, a situation foreseen by the town planners. Provision for parking was incorporated into street design and its accompanying network of underpasses and footbridges was a key aspect of the vision for the town. Children growing up in Cumbernauld never had to cross a road. We never had to, but we did.

By the mid-1970s, there was such a concern about us endangering our lives on the town's carriageways, that the CDC embarked upon a campaign of terror to save us from ourselves. A man from the CDC came to school to speak to us. We sat cross-legged in the gym to listen, but rather than give us a lecture on how we should use bridges, he told us monsters lived at the sides of the road and any child attempting to cross the road was liable to be caught and eaten alive.

It was exciting stuff, especially as he told us monsters hunting children left footprints behind. The gym was buzzing and, straight after school, the Boss Girl and I went straight to the bus stop at the top of our street to look for evidence. Sure enough, we found a set of footprints on the path. From them, we could tell the monsters walked barefoot and had huge feet with long toes and sharp, claw-like nails. We told each other the footprints weren't real, that they'd been painted there to scare little kids. All the same, when the Boss Girl wasn't looking, I took a nervous glance at the trees and bushes surrounding us. Anything could be lurking there, watching us, waiting to pounce.

But it wasn't the monsters at the side of the road I had to worry about.

Chapter XVIII.

Here Be Monsters

Going out in the car usually meant something good was happening. We were going to the coast. We were visiting my granny and grandad. We were going to the Kelvingrove to see the dinosaurs. But there were other times, like when a family day out had been planned but my mum wanted to hang out the washing before we left, which meant waiting for the machine to finish its cycle, which meant we were all ready and waiting to go but couldn't, which meant my dad went into a bad mood.

By the time we were packed in the car, he would be carrying his bad mood like a thunderstorm, his brow dark and heavy, while my mother oozed permafrost, her lips thin and tight. The joy would be sucked out of the day before we had even left the street.

Despite occasional thunderstorms and permafrost, summer days out were fun, but summer nights could be murder as my parents were strict about bedtime. It killed me to be lying in bed, sun streaming through the window while, out in the street, I could hear the other kids still out playing. I would whine to be allowed to stay up.

Just five more minutes, pleeeeease.

The flipside of their draconian *Get to bed now* rule was that it was all the more exciting when I was allowed to stay up late, and even more exciting when this meant going out in the car, with the headlights and streetlights and shroud of night.

On one occasion, we were going for a meal to celebrate something happening in the adult world. A new job perhaps. Usually, my mum sat in the front and my sister and I were in the back. But, because our pretend auntie and uncle were with us, my sister was in the back, wedged between my mother and Auntie Margo, and I was in the front, wearing my tartan skirt, white ankle socks, and red Clarks shoes, sitting on the knee of the man we called Uncle Alastair.

The adults were talking and laughing, the sound filling the car, wrapping itself around me like a warm blanket. It was one of those fleeting moments, a blip of happiness, the kind you're liable to forget. Except this moment stayed with me, to be relived over and again because, right in the middle of the laughter, Uncle Allastair slid his hand up my thighs, then wormed his fingers between my legs and into my pants.

In that moment, everything changed.

Of course, I didn't know that at the time. I didn't know the repercussions of what he did in that moment and what he would do in the months to come would ricochet through my life, leaving guilt, torment and self-loathing in their trail. And I didn't know about the bad choices I'd make in the future because my head was fucked. And it all started right there.

I didn't know anything. I didn't even have the words to describe what he was doing to me. I didn't shout out. I didn't tell my dad, who was sitting right beside me. I didn't tell my mum, who was sitting right behind me.

I froze.

I froze and he carried on.

We went for the meal. I sat at the table. Sitting nicely. Being a good girl. Trying to process what had just happened to me while he laughed with my parents, a monster hiding in plain sight. On the way home, he did it again.

Lying in the double bed I shared with my sister, I felt the burn of shame on my face. Although I couldn't articulate what he'd done, I knew it was wrong and that right there was the start of the guilt.

For years that turned into decades, I blamed myself, asking myself what I did to encourage him. Did I send him signals? Did I somehow convey to him that it was okay for him to do this to me? Did he think I wanted it to happen? Did I lead him on? Maybe I deserved it.

While I was blaming myself for years that turned into decades, I forgot that I was an eight-year-old in Clarks shoes and ankle socks and he was a 50-year-old man. He put the guilt in my head, making me promise not to tell. Saying that I'd be in trouble. He made me feel responsible, filling me with fear so I didn't make a fuss.

That night in the car was the first time. The last time it happened, they were at our house—drinking, talking, laughing with my parents. He drank whisky by then instead of cheap sherry, or at least he did in my father's company. He brought their carry-out to our house in a blue message bag. He'd raised his glass and said, *God bless the Duke of Argyll*, and laughed when it riled my father.

My bedroom was directly above the kitchen. My mum was in there, cleaning up. I could hear her moving things around and I heard his voice when he spoke to her.

Is it okay if I go upstairs to say goodnight to the girls?

In my bed, lying beside my little sister, I stiffened.

Yes, that's fine, my mum replied.

He'd groomed her most of all, filling a father-shaped void in her life.

I heard the creep of his footsteps coming up the stairs. The door opened slowly, gently even, admitting a fan of light from the hall, making a dark shadow of him. As he came into the room, the hall light caught the side of his face, illuminating his slicked-back white hair and glasses that glinted, shielding his eyes, and lips, narrow, wet and pink.

I slept on the side nearest the door. He told me to hush as he sat on the bed and slid his hand under the covers. I tried not to struggle as he pushed between my legs because I didn't want to wake my wee sister. I didn't want him to do to her what he was doing to me.

He had a hang nail and it hurt and I squirmed to get away. The bit I hated most of all was when he asked me for a kiss. I pecked him on the cheek hoping he'd go away.

No, give me a proper kiss.

He thrust his tongue into my mouth. I retched and panic took over. I writhed, bucking as I suffocated beneath his weight.

And then he was gone. It was just me and my wee sister sleeping beside me, and the voices coming up through the floor, chatting and laughing, and me upstairs, crying in the dark.

I didn't know that was the last time. Every time they were at our house or we were at theirs, I watched him sitting with his torpedo fingers wrapped around a whisky tumbler, and his trousers riding up to reveal hairless, pale skin between sock and hem, and I lived with the fear of it happening again.

He's dead now and I wish I believed in Hell.

Chapter XIX. 1974

The Ancient Romans built the Antonine Wall across the width of Scotland. They were also familiar with the comforts of central heating. 2,000 years later and only a short wander from the remains of that wall, we had a three-bar electric fire but Hell would have to freeze over before we could switch on all three bars at once.

Electricity was expensive and we weren't allowed to squander it. Using the immersion heater was seen as particularly expensive and so baths were not a daily occurrence. Heating the oven was also a costly affair and it was only switched on to cook multiple items at once. That was if we had the option to turn it on at all, for Britain was powered by coal, and stocks were running low.

OPEC (Organization of the Petroleum-Exporting Countries) was putting up the price of oil and the miners wanted the government to pay them for coal what they paid the Arabs for oil. When the government declined, the National Union of Miners (NUM) imposed an overtime ban. Pay talks also broke down with train drivers who moved coal around the country. When the Associated Society of Locomotive Engineers and Firemen (ASLEF) went on strike, almost all rail services were disrupted. Coal was predicted to run out by March.

On the 12th of December 1973, Conservative Prime Minister Edward Heath declared a state of emergency. The following day, he addressed the country on television:

We are asking you to cut down to the absolute minimum use of electricity for heating and other purposes in your homes. We are limiting the use of electricity to almost all factories, shops and offices to three days a week. We are imposing other restrictions. For example, on late night television. The reason is quite simple. At the moment, as a result of their ban on overtime, the coal miners are now sending to the power stations 60 tonnes of coal for every 100 they would normally do, so the stocks built up earlier in the year are falling.

The three-day week began on the 1st of January 1974. As darkness fell in that bleak mid-winter, I was thrilled by the prospect of living by candlelight four days a week. My sister and I huddled in blankets, entranced by the shadow animals Dad made on the wall. Admittedly, he had a limited repertoire; his pigeon looked remarkably like his seagull and it was only by his cooing or squawking I could tell the difference. It was fun, but all too soon our pleas of *Again, Daddy, again* were ignored and we were packed off to bed until it was time to get up again 15 hours later.

Along with a limited supply of electricity, there was a shortage of food and other essentials, including paraffin. This was bad news for me, as the only source of warmth we had in our bedroom was a paraffin heater.

Passing through Riddrie on the way back from visiting my grandparents, my dad noticed a queue outside a shop and pulled over. It turned out the shop had a supply of paraffin. Thinking he'd be recognised as a stranger in their midst so refused service, Dad gave me money and a gallon container kept in the boot for just such an occasion. He told me that if I was asked where I was from, I should say I was visiting my granny. It was like buying alcohol in Prohibition Era Chicago, or toilet rolls at the start of the COVID-19 pandemic.

I spent a fearful time in the queue wondering if I'd be interrogated and perhaps set upon as an interloper, but when I got to the counter, the man behind it managed to both serve me and barely notice me at the same time.

Our paraffin heater looked like a stunted *Doctor Who* Dalek but the blue flame burning in its belly provided comfort in the dark. By morning, its condensation was frozen in a solid sheet of ice covering the inside of the bedroom window. There was fun to be had in scraping and picking it off and occasional frissons of excitement when my finger briefly stuck to the ice.

We had no means of cooking other than the electric cooker and there must have been many difficulties involved in keeping the four of us fed, but although I remember doing my homework by candlelight, I don't recall any fuss about food. I suppose my mum just got on with it. I do remember that bread was in short supply and so was flour. When my dad came home with a couple bags, my mother baked her own bread on the days we had power, proving the dough in front of the living room fire. The magical, yeasty smell filled the house.

A general election was held on the 28th of February. Labour[21] won by four seats and, on the 5th of March, Harold Wilson formed a minority Labour government. Wilson settled with the miners and the State of Emergency ended on the 11th of March. The country went back to normal. At least whatever passed for normal in 1974.

We went on holiday to the Highlands that summer and spent two weeks in a caravan[22] in Helmsdale. Chickens were running around outside and my dad made endless jokes about catching one for the pot. My mum and I were chased by terns on a beach and, on another beach, I found a dead dog shark that I studied for a long time. My dad got boozed up and maudlin one night and told me about the babies my mum lost before she had me. I didn't know what to say to that.

I turned 10 a couple weeks after we got back and my parents gave me a party. My days of digging dirt had passed. Now I mostly played with other girls. Some games, such as hopscotch, five jacks and marbles that we played on metal sewer lids like a primitive version of Pac-Man I understood and enjoyed. Yet when it came to more complex girl games, especially ones played in time to rhythmic chants, I was lost.

The game of balls, where two hard balls were bounced against a wall in time to a series of songs required a level of eye–hand coordination that was beyond me.

The Big Ship Sails on the Alley-Alley-O, the Alley-Alley-O.

I was rubbish at Chinese ropes. These were made from hundreds of elastic bands tied together. Two people stretched them out and a series of jumps and twists were performed over and between them to yet more chants.

Ingle angle, silver bangle, ingle angle out.

---

[21] The two main political parties in Britain were the Conservatives (Tories), right of centre, and Labour, left of centre.
[22] The UK equivalent of the US trailer house.

My scissors jump was particularly woeful and I was even more terrible at skipping games, either coming in on the wrong beat or ruining the game altogether by getting my foot fankled in the rope.

Spanish lady, turn around, Spanish lady, touch the ground.

As if that wasn't enough, there were also the clapping games where we stood in a circle, clapping with various movements thrown in that each girl had to keep up with. Or in my case, not.

Who stole a kiss from the boy next door. Was it you, number one?

Who, me?
Yes, you.
Couldn't have been.
Then who?
Number two?
Who, me?
Yes, you.
Couldn't have been.
Then who?

And on and on and on.

Despite being rubbish at their games and never getting to grips with the complexities of girl rules, all my party guests were girls. They gave me birthday presents of googly-eyed Gonks and books and my first proper single, *Summerlove Sensation* by Bay City Rollers, Scotland's tartan-clad answer to The Osmonds. We played pass the parcel and pin the tail on the donkey and ate strawberry tarts made by my mum.

My parents gave me the 1970s version of a virtual reality headset: a View-Master. This was a 3D-effect slideshow you look through like a pair of binoculars. The slides came on thin reels. Although there were hundreds of reels available, I only ever had two and spent the next year looking at the same images of Mickey Mouse and Mount Kilimanjaro over again.

Ever the spectres at the feast, Auntie Margo and Uncle Allastair, gave me a Ladybird book about trees. I took it to school and lost it on the way.

Chapter XX. Dealing with Shit

Growing up is not a linear thing. The same time I was reading my first adult book, I was still reading Enid Blyton's *Famous Five* books and, alongside teen magazine *Jackie,* I continued to read *The Beano* and my wee sister's *Bimbo* annuals. I'd outgrown the children's library but they wouldn't let me into the adult section. Instead, I had to make do with the paperbacks that passed through our house. In this way I learned about incest and rape from *Peyton Place*, and was scandalised by *Drum*, one of Kyle Onstott's exploitation books about slave plantations. While the vivid descriptions of slavery intrigued and shocked me, the scene that dropped my jaw was when Drum had to use a communal toilet alongside a large woman who had no sense of modesty.

I couldn't put the book down and my father was outraged when he saw me reading it at the table. He went through the kitchen like a tornado, snatching the book away and throwing it on the counter, beside where my mother was ironing. I waited until he'd gone then asked her if I had to stop reading it. She didn't look at me when she answered.

Don't let your dad see.

Way before *Peyton Place* and *Drum*, there was *Jaws*. I was 10 when I ploughed through it, learning the word vagina along the way. I said in my head as *vah-jeen-a*. Years passed before I learned the correct pronunciation in sex education class at high school. Meanwhile, other words were being bandied around by boys at primary school: *fanny*[23]*, fud, hairy banjo.* One of the boys sang a song to another girl and me, pointing to the relevant parts of his body as he sang, *Bum tit tit, bum tit tit, play your hairy banjo.*

My face went lava hot while the other girl laughed herself silly. My cheeks were similarly scalded when I shared a

---

[23] Fanny in the UK means vulva or vagina, as do fud and hairy banjo.

changing cubicle with the Boss Girl at swimming lessons. She snuck a peek and whispered,

You've got hair.

I was too young for dealing with this shit.

The separation of girls from boys at my 10th birthday party continued at school, when we were given a choice of crafts. I was not allowed to choose balsa wood. *Balsa wood is for boys*, the teacher told me. Instead of playing with hammers and saws, I had to learn how to sew. I hated it and only took pleasure in doing it badly. I was told to redo my work so many times that I never finished making the turquoise nylon underskirt I would never have worn anyway.

They began to separate us at gym, the boys going off to play football on the blaes pitch while the girls were suddenly picking teams for netball in the hall. I was confused. How did all the other girls know how to play this game that appeared out of nowhere? They knew the rules. They knew what the mysterious letters on the bibs meant. They even knew how to pass the stupid ball around. How could they know all of this when I knew nothing? I experienced the same feelings again a couple years later in the sex education lesson at high school.

This comprised a film followed by a Q&A with a teacher, girls separated from boys. The film was a revelation to me, and I was glad the lights were dimmed so that no-one could see my scarlet face. I was still stunned as we filed out of the theatre. I had no idea that it was the penis that did it. After what *Uncle* Allastair had done to me, I was convinced that it was all about fingers.

In the classroom, our guidance teacher said, *I doubt any of you learned anything you didn't already know.*

There was much knowing laughter and nodding in response. I nodded and laughed along with the other girls but I was still goggle-eyed and thinking, *Everyone already knew this stuff, really?* I mean, come on. Sex, netball, where did they learn this shit?

There were so many complex rules wrapped up in being a girl. The Boss Girl was always quick to point out when I'd made an error, with the other girls sniggering at my stupidity when my joke fell flat or when I said that I liked something we weren't supposed to like. I was too young for that shit. It was a minefield. Being a boy seemed so much simpler. No wonder Georgina in the *Famous Five* books made everyone call her George. George was allowed to go off and have adventures with the boys while Anne the girl was left behind to clean the cave and make the tea.

Being a boy didn't just seem easier, it seemed better. Gran Brannigan gave extra chocolates to my boy cousins *because they are boys*, she said. Boys, the message seemed to be, were more deserving. Or, put another way, girls were less deserving. Everywhere I looked, the point was hammered home.

Our primary school teachers were almost all women, but the headteachers in charge were men. Pubs could refuse to serve women because they were women. Pubs were for men. Rape within marriage was legal. Men were entitled to conjugal rights. We were told that girls said no when they meant yes.

Our job was to sit nice, play nice and, most of all, look nice. Women who didn't look nice were mocked and jeered. On the sitcom *On the Buses*, Olive's husband called her an ugly cow. The insult was rewarded by a burst of canned laughter. Abusing women was comedy gold.

When I was 12 and on my way to the corner shop, a man yelled at me, *No bad tits for a wee lassie*. I was mortified, my face radiating more heat than 20 suns. There's no way I should have been dealing with that shit. Men had the right to look and leer, to comment and touch. At school, at home, and out on the street, men were in charge of everything.

After my sister started school, my mother got a job in a factory making telephone components. That was just a job. What excited her was when she later trained as an auxiliary nurse on a geriatric ward. Working with old people gave her a great deal of satisfaction and purpose. Their dignity mattered to her and she loved the job.

That year, she sat my sister and me down and asked us if we minded her working on Christmas morning so that she could give the old people their breakfasts. She explained that some of them were lonely and didn't have people to visit and she'd be home in the afternoon to spend the rest of Christmas

Day with us. I said I didn't mind and then forgot all about it. That Christmas, my mum was home all day.

I didn't know for years to come that my dad tried to guilt her about working on Christmas Day and, when that didn't work, he made it too difficult for her to do the job she loved. He wanted her life organised to suit his needs and wore her down until she gave up a potential career doing something that fulfilled her. Instead, she became a cleaner in the toonie.

Men were in charge of everything.

Chapter XXI. **Roots**

It is late afternoon, and the sky is already a dark matte mass. All the light, all the glimmer, comes from the crisscross of streets below. Around me, people are teeming along the pavement, moving with purpose and precision. They know where they are going, but me—I am drifting, tethered only by my father's fierce grasp. Crossing the road, the people half run, half walk, trying to beat the lights and the rumble of traffic that follows. Buses rattle by, belching half-digested diesel, their windows running with condensation on the inside and caked with grime without. The ground has been glossed by rain. Tarmac and paving slabs reflect shop lights, traffic lights, head lights, streetlights. My hand is small and warm within my father's encompassing grip. He's making sure that I don't get swept away or knocked over or lost within the deep shadow and bright illumination of the bustle. And then he nudges me. *Look.* And there, high above it all, flashing in bright neon colours, is the Barr's Irn-Bru[24] sign, its vivacious glow containing all the lure and promise of the city.

I loved Glasgow. It seemed like such a real place to me, a proper place. I was jealous that my parents came from there in a way that I did not. They were rooted in the city while I was growing up in a town recently invented—a place with no mythology to call its own. It felt like I didn't properly come from or belong anywhere.

In a school register brimming with Scottish surnames—*Mackenzie, Bryce, Murray, Macaulay, Lennox, Moncur, Lawson, Gillespie*—my name stood out. Teachers asked, *Are your grandparents French?*

---

[24] This soft drink was originally called Barr's Iron Brew. Although it did contain iron, the drink wasn't brewed so, with the advent of labelling regulations after WWII, the name was changed to Irn-Bru. One of Irn-Bru's most famous advertising taglines is *Made in Scotland from girders.*

I shook my head. No-one in my family was French. Everyone was from Glasgow. It was my grandad who eventually told me that his family—my family—weren't French but Lithuanian. Although we spent a lot of time together, he talked very little about personal matters—our conversations mostly revolved around films and books—but he did tell me that his parents came from Lithuania and that he had been born with the name Zekyll.

Zekyll, like Jekyll and Hyde, was how he said it.

He said they changed the name to the French one because his sister, Betty, needed a fancy name for her hostess job. I wish I'd asked him more but that time has long gone and so I've done some digging of my own.

The Forty Years of Darkness was an era of severe repression in Lithuania. From 1864 to 1904, draconian measures were imposed by the Czarist Russians in response to an attempted rebellion by the occupied Lithuanians. During this time, the Russian government banned the printing in Latin script of Lithuanian books, journals, and newspapers. In response, the Lithuanians refused to print and read books printed in the Russian Cyrillic alphabet. The result was four decades of educational and cultural darkness. My great grandparents were born in Lithuania during this period. According to family myth, they came from the capital, Vilna (now called Vilnius), the evidence for this being that my great auntie was once heard declaring, *Everything was left in Vilna!*

From their marriage certificate, I know that Jonas was born in 1872 to Marie and Ludovic Zabel. Ludovic was a farm servant. The occupation of mothers was not recorded. Jonas's wife, Catherine, was born in 1878 to William and Yoniesska Yuodivris. William was a shoemaker.

Jonas and Catherine were part of a wave of migration from Eastern Europe to Scotland that took place from the 1880s until the outbreak of war in 1914. The route from East to West was long and perilous. Most Lithuanians crossed borders illegally before setting sail from one of the German ports such as Hamburg or Bremen. It is possible that Scotland was not Jonas and Catherine's intended final destination. Most European emigrants at that time planned to seek their fortune in the United States, where the very streets were said to be paved with gold, but direct passage to the USA cost five times as much as a ticket to Scotland and so Scotland was often used as a stepping-stone between the North Sea and the Atlantic Ocean. Whatever dreams Jonas and Catherine may have had, they got no further than Glasgow.

The main reasons for emigration from Lithuania at that time were economic hardships, military conscription for all Lithuanian men (with no limit on the time served), and persecution by the Russians on racial, religious, or political grounds. Any or all of these could be why Jonas and Catherine ended up in the Gorbals area of Glasgow.

In the late 1920s into the 1930s, the Gorbals became infamous for its razor gangs[25], but in the 19th century, its shoddily built tenements became home to people fleeing persecution. In addition to thousands of immigrants seeking work in the city, including a sizeable population of Lithuanians, there were also a great many Highlanders who had been cleared from their homes and land[26].

By the time the 20th century rolled around, the tenements were rat-infested slums with as many as 10 people living in one room. Filthy communal toilets were used by up to 30 people. The meaning of Glasgow is "dear green place", but the only greenery in the Gorbals was the corporation burial ground and, with such appalling living conditions, the area supported a grim abundance of undertakers. Life was tough for those who lived there, so perhaps it is not surprising that the Gorbals was the birthplace of the fighter Benny Lynch, considered by many to be Scotland's greatest ever boxer. The Gorbals was also the birthplace of my Great Auntie Betty.

---

[25] Gangs running wild in the East End and South Side of Glasgow, named after their weapon of choice.

[26] The Highland Clearances was an atrocity that still scars the Highlands to this day. Highlanders were forcibly evicted from their homes by landowners to make way for more profitable sheep. In many cases, their homes were burned behind them so that they could not return. So many Highlanders made their way to Glasgow, that the Central Station railway bridge became known as the Hielanman's Umbrella, *Hielan* being a Glaswegian contraction of Highland.

Betty, the oldest of my grandad's siblings, was born in the Gorbals in 1900, her birth marked on the register as illegitimate. Though Betty lived until the age of 97, I never met her or any of my grandad's siblings.

Jonas and Catherine were married in Glasgow nine days after Betty's birth. Jonas was 28, Catherine 22. Their address was 125 Thistle Street in the Gorbals, now the site of not very much. Jonas gave his occupation as tailor (journeyman) and each of them marked the marriage certificate with their X.

While many settled in the Gorbals and the East End of Glasgow, the greatest area of settlement for Lithuanian immigrants was Bellshill in Lanarkshire. Lithuanians were routinely referred to as Poles and Bellshill became known as Little Poland. In this community, the traditions, language, and culture of the old country were kept alive, helped by the publication of a newspaper printed in Lithuanian. Meanwhile, many Lithuanians who settled elsewhere were intent on assimilation. They anglicised their names, spoke in English, and adopted the customs of their new homeland. Some never spoke Lithuanian even at home. My family fell into this category.

Despite so many Lithuanians settling in Scotland, only 11 people with the surname Zekyll are recorded in the whole of the country, these being my great grandparents and their 9 children. The only Yuodivris on record is my great grandmother. As Jonas and Catherine marked their marriage certificate with an X, indicating that they were illiterate, it's highly likely that the spellings of their names were the best guess of the registrar. It seems that everything was left in Vilna after all. Even our family name.

My great uncle Jonas Zekyll was born in Glasgow's East End in 1901. He died in 1980. When told of his brother's death, my grandad responded with a typically stoic, single syllable, *Aye*. The next child, Wallace, was born in 1903. A colliery hewer[27], he died in Glasgow's Royal Infirmary while

---

[27] The person loosening coal from the bed. A tough, dirty job.

undergoing an operation on an enlarged thyroid (described as a toxic goitre on the corrected entry to his death certificate).

Catherine gave birth to her fourth child in 1904, a daughter also named Catherine, who died of bronchitis just two weeks later. By 1906, Jonas and Catherine had moved to The Calton, an area of extreme poverty in Glasgow's East End. It was here that Catherine gave birth to John Zekyll. John, a stoker in the Merchant Navy, was last seen alive on the 21st of November 1942. His body was recovered from the River Clyde, at Prince's Dock, Govan, on the 19th of December. Cause of death: drowning.

By the time my great uncle Peter was born in May 1908, Jonas and Catherine were living at their final address on Dalmarnock Road, Bridgeton, in Glasgow's East End. Peter died when he was 17 months old, having suffered from acute broncho-pneumonia for 10 days. At the time of his death, Catherine was already six months pregnant with her next child, a daughter called Nellie. Nellie later became a shorthand typist and court stenographer. In 1940, she married Campbell Wilkins, a motor lorry driver. She died in 1992.

Catherine's eighth child, Josephine, was born in February 1913. She died on the 31st of July, aged just 5 months, after suffering whooping cough for 28 days and broncho-pneumonia for four days. On the 3rd of September 1914, Catherine gave birth to her ninth and final child, my grandfather. Born during the early months of the First World War, he was the last person to be born with the name Zekyll.

Catherine died four years later at the age of 40 in the second wave of Spanish Flu in October 1918. The pandemic killed an estimated 50 million people across the globe, with over 17,000 deaths in Scotland, these mostly from ill-nourished working-class families. The first outbreak in the early summer of 1918 caused deaths mainly among the very young, the elderly and those already sick[28]. The second struck

---

[28] The COVID-19 pandemic struck while I was working on this book. There was a lot of fear and apprehension, particularly at the beginning. We didn't know how bad this virus was going to be or what the government would do in response, but we knew something was coming.

in autumn and was much more severe. Half of the fatalities this time were among people between the ages of 20 and 40, my great grandmother among them. The third outbreak came in early 1919. The mortality rate was high with reports of healthy adults dying within a day of catching the virus.

We Scots like to think of ourselves as friendly, welcoming people. Whatever truth there is in that statement today, it wasn't the case in the late 19th and early 20th centuries when bigotry, suspicion, and hostility towards immigrants in general, and Lithuanian immigrants in particular, were the norm. Following the introduction of the Aliens Act in 1905, Jonas was issued with an alien book to be carried with him at all times. It held his personal details including his address and where he got married, and was inspected annually by the local constabulary, a practice that went on until the late 1950s.

The term alien was also used in an unofficial and derogatory way. My granny used it as a slur to insult my grandad when she was angry with him. *What do you know? You're just an alien.*

It was after Catherine's death that the family name was changed. The period between the World Wars was turbulent and so it is very likely that the Zekylls wanted to appear less foreign, less alien. But why choose a French surname over something more obviously Scottish? As my grandad speculated, it most likely comes down to Betty.

Betty was 18 when her mother died, and she seems to have been something of a dynamic force. Before she became a night club hostess, she was one of the Tiller Girls, high-kicking precision dancers performing in theatres around the world, including on Broadway and at the London Palladium and the Folies Bergère in Paris.

During the COVID-19 pandemic, our younger daughter was a student in Dundee. We were worried about her being stranded there by herself so her sister made the 400-mile trip overnight to bring her home. The country went into lockdown three days later. Just over 100 years after my great grandmother died of the Spanish Flu, I couldn't help but wonder if I would meet a similar fate in the 21st century.

The girls in each troupe were matched for height and weight, and, if ethnicity came into it, perhaps Betty thought a name with a hint of French glamour was a good career move. Her father took her lead and the rest of the family, from 17-year-old Jonas to my four-year-old grandad, followed suit.

Between their marriage in 1900 and the birth of their fifth child in 1906, Jonas and Catherine changed address at least four times, but, by 1908, they had settled at 305 Dalmarnock Road. It was in this tenement that Catherine gave birth to her last four children, two of whom died in infancy. It was also here, no doubt in the same bed where she'd birthed her children, that Catherine herself died. The flat continued to be Jonas's home until he died of bowel cancer and cardiac failure in 1934. So many births and deaths under one roof. So much love and loss and heartache in one solitary tenement flat, and no doubt similar pain and occasional moments of joy echoed throughout the neighbouring flats and tenements.

The tenements were knocked down in the 1960s and '70s. Not many mourned the slum dwellings with shared lavatories, communal taps, a thriving rat population and little in the way of privacy, but, when they went, so too did the community. Nothing much stands on the site today. Where once people lived and worked, and loved and grieved, there is now only a bleak stretch of road.

The descendants of those fleeing persecution were dispersed to new homes. Modern houses were erected in the area, but it's possible some families who lived in Dalmarnock Road tenements moved to Cumbernauld for the new town.

Chapter XXII.

Grandad

I saw a lot more of my grandad after my dad won the pools and we got a car. As well as our day trips, we began going on holiday at Easter, renting a caravan in Anstruther on the Fife coast. My dad packed me, my sister, our granny and grandad, and sometimes my cousin into the car with our luggage and a box of groceries, driving us up and then coming back the next weekend to take us home.

In a world of vanilla, a rum 'n' raisin ice-cream cone from the shop at the campsite was a special treat. We walked around the harbour, looking at the fishing boats and one of my secret delights was reading the harbour notice about rabies. I was excited at the remote possibility of a rabid dog leaping from a visiting boat. My sister and I would clamber around the rocks at the shore, looking for crabs and collecting shells and sea glass. Once, when my cousin was with us, he kicked a limpet from a rock and I, who was in the habit of collecting buckets of frogs and keeping bees as pets in jars, cried at his cruelty. In the evening, the caravan dripped with steam from boiling crabs and whelks as we played cards and dominoes.

My grandad began spending more time with us in Cumbernauld. My dad would pick him up and he'd stay for a few days. He and my dad watched the snooker on our rented black-and-white telly. I still remember some of the players of the day: Hurricane Higgins, Terry Griffiths, Ray Reardon. Ray Reardon was my favourite, as his widow's peak and distinctive grin earned him the nickname Dracula. If my parents went out for the night, my sister and I played at hairdressers with Grandad as the customer. He'd sit there quite the thing, watching telly, as we mixed talcum powder into a paste with water and used it to spike his hair like Oor Wullie[29].

---

[29] Oor Wullie is a mischievous cartoon strip character whose antics were depicted in *The Sunday Post* and biennial books published for Christmas. Oor Wullie has short, spiky hair, tackety boots and black dungarees, and

We went for many walks together, just Grandad and me, walking for hours all over the town, from Ravenswood to Seafar, concrete flagstones beneath our feet, crossing the snaky bridge to Kildrum, then onto Cumbernauld Park, where bare trees with twiggy branches reached towards a cold, blue spring sky. He liked to get dressed up when he went out. *Joe the Toff*, he'd say when he was suited and booted, big black overcoat on. This was the same coat that served as an extra blanket at home in Carntyne.

We loved the old Universal horror films, especially *Dracula*. We imitated Bela Lugosi for each other. *Listen to them, the children of the night—what sweet music they make.* And our favourite, *I don't drink... wine*, complete with dramatic pause. In later years, when Grandad was having some physical problems that made it appear he was losing his mental faculties, he quietly ranted to me, *They think I'm catching flies*. This a reference to the Renfield character in *Dracula* who is locked up in a lunatic asylum.

We loved reading horror stories and exchanged gruesome details from the books we'd read, like the Pan Horror Stories series and *The Rats* by James Herbert. For Granddad's birthday one year, I did a huge drawing of a giant rat with blood dripping from its incisors and **Happy Birthday Grandad** written underneath. I remember once seeing my parents spotting us in deep discussion. Amused, they nudged each other, no idea of the grisly matters we were discussing.

It was on one of our long walks when it was just the two of us that my grandad lost his temper. This was a rare occurrence, a real jolt. We were passing a shop in Carbrain and I asked if I could get a sweetie. He started ranting at me. I can't remember the words—just how horrible I felt. It was years before I realised that his anger was caused by embarrassment because he had no money in his pocket.

I must have been a peculiarly naïve child. I knew his coat was used as a blanket on his bed but I didn't equate that with poverty. During winter, the window in my bedroom was

---

famously sits on an upturned bucket. His friends were Fat Bob, Soapy Soutar and Wee Eck, and a pet mouse called Jeemy.

frequently coated with ice on the inside, so keeping warm in bed made sense to me. It didn't occur to me that we weren't particularly well-off.

Though she was four years younger than me, my sister had a better grasp of the situation. Occasionally when we were visiting, one or other of our grandparents would give us a coin each. I was always super excited by this and put it in my pocket straightaway, thinking about sweeties I could buy. I was all for taking anything I was given, be it money, a Club biscuit or a wee pencil from the bookies. My sister was made of better stuff. She'd take the money then slip it down the side of the settee where they'd find it later. She knew they were poor in a way that I didn't. To me, they were adults, adults were in charge, so I thought that they chose to live the way they did with no carpets and not much of anything else.

Whenever we'd gone out for the day, either up to the Fife Coast at Aberdour, or down the west coast to the Maidens, my grandad would always sigh on the return journey, *Back to Paradise*. I thought it was just one of his ways and would laugh. He'd laugh too but not because it was funny.

I liked all his wee ways, like calling the messages *the rations*. When he was in a good mood, he'd sing the song "When You and I Were Young, Maggie" to my granny, and, when he was exasperated, he'd say, *Heaven's sake, Maggie!* He went to the library several times every week, Louis L'Amour cowboy books being a favourite along with the horror stories and classics. On the few occasions I was in a pub with him, he drank a *hauf 'n' a hauf*—a half pint of beer with a whisky chaser. He liked plain food, Scotch Broth, mince and tatties. He had no teeth. Unlike my granny, he never wore falsers, but, his gums were so hard, he could bite into an apple. He liked to put a bet on at the bookies but, like my father, he only ever bet small amounts, 10 pence each way and the like, and he enjoyed going to the dog racing at Shawfield.

When Grandad was a youth, he used to go to the Panopticon Music Hall in Glasgow's Trongate. In its time, the Panopticon included a freak show, waxworks, zoo, and, of course, the theatre. An audience of around 1,500 people crammed into the auditorium, and, there being no facilities available, urinated where they could, often where they stood, this having the unintended consequence of preserving the wood. The place was described as having an insufferably offensive smell. I like to think my grandad played his part.

Stan Laurel made his first stage appearance at the Panopticon, an experience I was disappointed to learn my grandad had missed out on as he wasn't yet born, although it is possible that he saw the heaviest woman in the world, *LUCY MOORE, The American Fat Girl. Weight 46 st.*[30] *THE RECORD FAT GIRL—STILL GROWING.* Lucy sat on a chair while Panopticon punters walked around her, astounded by her girth from every angle.

Black market interests aside, my grandad was a general labourer when he married my granny, and, as mentioned, during the war he was a Gunner in the Royal Artillery. After that he was a street vendor, calling out the headlines as he sold the *Evening Times* in Glasgow, and then he ended up in jail for cutting a man's throat. The way my grandad told it to me, the man was choking and, while my grandad was cutting his tie to save him, he accidentally cut the man's throat. I heard a more likely version from my uncle. Newspaper vendors carried small knives to cut the string wrapped around the newspaper bundles. According to my uncle, the man tried to steal my grandad's takings. My grandad instinctively went to grab him, forgetting he was holding his knife, and the man ended up with his throat cut. Either way or something in between or otherwise, a man's throat was cut and my grandad was done for assault and banged up in Saughton Prison in Edinburgh.

When Myreside Place was condemned, my granny and grandad were among the last to be moved out of the tenement. One night when my grandad was going up the stairs, he heard people moving around in the empty flat below. Worried about the place being set on fire, he investigated and was hit over the head with a lead pipe for his troubles. By the time he was bandaged up in the Royal Infirmary, Dad was chasing around

---

[30] A stone is an imperial measure of weight equivalent to 14 lbs, so Lucy would have weighed 644 pounds.

Carntyne, seeking vengeance with a blunt instrument in his hand. It's probably just as well he never found the culprits.

They were moved to a much smaller tenement flat in Oatlands. Within walking distance of Shawfield and right across the street from Richmond Park, it consisted of just two rooms: a combined living room and kitchen, plus a bedroom, with a small bathroom wedged between. With high ceilings but not much floor space, the proportions were all wrong, but it was clean and newly done up, with a security door at the close entrance and a back court with neat bin cellars beside shrub beds. It didn't stay that way for long.

Over a period of a few short years, the sand-blasted tenements and their well-ordered back courts deteriorated into slums. Instead of taking their rubbish down to the bins, people threw it out of windows. Seagulls swooped on the rotting food and my grandparents were distressed to see rats running along the gutters of the opposite building. The security door was kicked open and left hanging off its hinges. Graffiti appeared, and not the kind you'd call street art. Instead of being a place where you'd go for a stroll to feed the swans, the park became a place to avoid.

Although I knew him as a man with a twinkle in his eye, I saw enough of my grandad to know he could be hard, and he was definitely a rogue. When my granny was pregnant, he had an affair with a woman whose name later flew through the air when drink had been drunk. On the flipside, my granny hadn't lacked for company when my grandad had been in jail.

Despite the jail and the poverty and all the shite of life that came their way, they stuck it out and were married for 53 years when Granny died. Grandad then moved to a sheltered housing complex in Govan, where he experienced a new lease of life in his wee flat. There were various illnesses along the way but he died peacefully in his sleep at the age of 83 and nobody thought he was catching flies.

Chapter XXIII.

Summer of '76

The summer of '76 was a scorcher. It was all blue skies, sunshine and Elton John and Kiki Dee on the radio, singing "Don't Go Breaking My Heart". I'd finished primary school, was excited about going to high school, and we were going on holiday to Cornwall.

My dad had got a new car from the scrappy—new to us, that is. We were on our third car by then. After the Ford Escort, there was the Wolseley, a lovely, big motor that my sister and I called the James Bond Car because it had a cigarette lighter and an armrest we could pull down in the backseat. The dashboard was walnut and we all thought it was really posh. Our new car was a yellow Ford Cortina.

It was over 500 miles from Cumbernauld to our destination in Cornwall and the Cortina broke down in dramatic style about 10 miles from home, with orange steam billowing from under the bonnet. My dad joined the Royal Automobile Club (RAC) from a roadside phone, the car was fixed and we went on our way, but the traffic was bumper to bumper on the motorway, engines were overheating and we were crawling along. We eventually pulled into a motorway service station and slept in the car for a couple of hours before leaving again in the early morning.

All told, it took 16 hours to get to the farmhouse guesthouse with the sloping floors, but it was worth it. There was a beach nearby with golden sand and, almost every day, I stood in the sea, waiting for the big rollers to come in so that I could jump up and ride over them like a cork. Other holidaymakers were doing the same and all of us were laughing in the sun. Three weeks later, I started high school[31].

---

[31] In the UK, children attend primary school for seven years (roughly from ages 5 to 12) then secondary school for 4 to 6 years. These days, it's the norm to stay at secondary for 5 or 6 years but, in the '70s, the

I want to hug the young girl I was at the swing park that morning. It wasn't long after my twelfth birthday and I was so excited about starting high school that I woke up early and took myself for a wander. The entire summer had been sunshine and blue skies and this mid-August morning was no different. I thought high school was going to be an amazing experience. We were going to have French lessons and I was naïve enough to think I'd soon be fluent.

My optimistic outlook chimed neatly with that of the school rector, Mr Arnott. He was a tall, slender man, who wore black robes to address the first-year assembly later that morning. He talked about the 1963 assassination of American president John F. Kennedy and how everyone remembered where they were when they heard the news. He suggested that, likewise, everyone at the assembly would remember the momentous day they started at Greenfaulds High School. He was right, I did. Though not for the reasons he had in mind.

There was a plaque at the main entrance of the school, saying that it had opened in 1971. Though the building was only five years old, I had no sense of its newness. 1971 was another planet. I was a little kid back then, excited to hear the ragman[32] playing his bugle to announce his presence in the street, though I was timid about approaching him. He looked like someone who might bundle a little kid into a sack but the lure of the treasure he kept in his van overcame my fear. I mithered my mother for old clothes I could take out to him and was delighted to receive a balloon on a stick in exchange. My mother wasn't too impressed but she was better pleased another time when I returned with a red yo-yo. My mouth hung open when she proceeded to work it like a pro, doing tricks like walking the dog.

---

vast majority of students left secondary school after 4 years at the age of 16. Secondary schools in Cumbernauld were called high schools.

[32] Rag men (or rag-and-bone men) went about the streets, collecting unwanted household goods to sell to merchants. Traditionally, this was done on foot or pony and cart, but, by the late 1960s, the rag men I saw were driving small vans.

After Boss Girl told me that bin men[33] threw stray kids into the back of the lorry, I was even more wary of them. It was one of those urban myths that I didn't quite believe—like how an apple tree would grow inside you if you swallowed the pips, or that swallowed chewing gum would strangle your stomach—but it wasn't worth taking the chance. So whenever the bin lorry came down the street, I went into the house.

The high school was so big and solid, it felt like it must always have been there. Like the rest of the town, it was built in the brutalist style. The main body consisted of two cuboid blocks, each three storeys high, off-set and connected by a central staircase. A cluster of stark, geometric forms made up a third section that housed the swimming pool, games hall, technical department, and the theatre where we were addressed by Mr Arnott.

The theatre was packed full. A line of adults, our registration teachers, stood behind the rector. Mostly, they were an arrangement of skirts and blouses, jackets and ties, but a few stood out. Aside from Mrs Mack, the French teacher who was dressed in wildly flared trousers and with dark hair framing her face, the different ones turned out to be art teachers. Mr David in jeans, Mr Bush in dungarees, and a purple-suited man with a blaze of white-blond hair. This was Mr MacRae. He would become an important figure in my life, but not for a few years yet.

The classes were assigned alphabetically. I was in 1E. As we were filing out of the theatre, I was dunted hard in the back by a girl who didn't like the way I looked and didn't give a shit about letting me know it. The first hint of worse to come.

Except for Seafar, each primary school fed its students into one of the three high schools, but the kids from Seafar were split into two groups, half going to Cumbernauld High, and half to Greenfaulds, where I was. In addition to lessening the chance of being in classes with people I knew, it meant that I would never again see the friends who had gone to the other school, but at least I had Maureen.

---

[33] Known in the US as garbagemen or trashmen.

Maureen became my best friend by default. I didn't know her until my last year at primary school, when we were put in the same group in class, but we became friendly over the year. We lived in the same neighbourhood and hung out through that summer. We'd walked to school together that morning and now, swamped in a turbulent sea of new faces, I looked to her as a human life raft. But this being Scotland, with its plethora of Mcs and Macs, there were entire classes made up of people whose surname began with M and, while Maureen was one of them, I was not. I was cast adrift.

As it turned out, there were two girls and two boys in 1E who also had gone to Seafar. The other girls immediately became best friends and so I began my high school career sitting by myself. The boys in the class were sussing each other out when Ryan, one of the Seafar boys, made a point of announcing that I was a swot. He was no dunce himself—it was a classic deflection move on his part, one my swift and witty retort of *I am not*, was powerless against. The moment he opened his mouth, I was branded.

If you think being called a swot wasn't that big a deal, you clearly did not go to a Scottish comprehensive school in the 1970s. There was no such thing as geek chic. Urban Dictionary's definition of swot states that *to be called a swot is a horrible, undesirable humiliation for the victim*. I would say that *horrible, undesirable humiliation* is putting it mildly.

Being branded a swot coupled with having no friends in class meant, from day one, I was fair game for pushing around. The tough girls wearing fashionable platform shoes and box pleat skirts sneered and called me names (*Ugly boot! Fat cow!*) as they shunted me in the corridors and PE changing rooms, mocking me more when I lost my balance and lurched in a way that they found amusing. If you're wondering why I didn't stick up for myself, it was because I was shit scared of them, and with good reason. Within my first couple days at high school, I'd witnessed two older girls knock hell out of each other. Grabbing hair, clawing, kicking—it was a no-holds barred vicious scrap and I didn't want it happening to me.

Occasionally, I'd see some poor sod volleyed along the corridors with a **kick me** sign taped to his back, kids laughing as they duly obeyed the instruction while the hapless victim wondered why everyone was giving him a hard time.

I was special. I didn't need a sign.

As well as being shoved around by the tough girls in my class, I was fresh blood for the terrifying older girls. There's a hell of a difference in size between the average 12-year-old and a hulking 15-year-old, especially when the hulking 15-year-old is wearing 4-inch platforms. If I happened to drift into their line of sight, they'd give me a shove in an offhand, almost casual manner. I got used to that and just kind of stumbled on. When it was a deliberate act, I knew all about it. They'd really whack into me, malicious. I was on the receiving end of one of these attacks after committing a crime of fashion. You'd have thunk this would have been nigh on impossible in the 1970s, but I managed it.

Look at that stupid idiot wearing a bra and a vest.

There was a herd of us moving into the school after the buzzer went and I wasn't even sure it was me she was talking about until I went flying.

I didn't like the way my body was changing, mainly because of the reaction I got from grown men. When my mother insisted I had to start wearing a bra, I clung obstinately to my vest. The brilliantly conceived see-through school blouses made my undergarment choices plain for all to see. I ditched the vest after the shoving and, not long after that, I refused to wear anything resembling a school uniform.

All of that was yet to come. All I'd experienced in my first hour at high school was a hard shove in the back, isolation, and being called a swot, but Mr David, our registration teacher, was about to compound my woes. He'd given us forms to fill in and, after we handed them back, he picked out mine as having the best handwriting. The rewards were rich. On top of my swottiness now cast in iron, I was tasked with writing the absence slip when Mr David did the register every morning and then taking it from class to class for the teachers. *Brilliant.*

Before we were let loose in the school, Mr David took us through our timetable. He gave us useful information such as telling us that home economics was known as home eccy.

Home eccy—sewing and cooking—was for girls of course, while boys went to techy drawing, woodwork and metalwork classes. What he didn't tell us about was the word *beamer*. When you blushed that was a beamer. When you had a beamer, people pointed at you and yelled *BEAMER*, which had the effect of extending and deepening the beamer. *BEAMER* was yelled at me a lot.

Sewing aside, the timetable sounded really exciting. I couldn't wait to learn French and was beside myself with glee at the prospect of learning science. Bunsen burners! Test tubes! Magnesium ribbon! The big, beautiful periodic table with the elements all organised in their little boxes, and the chairs with their own little flip desks. I'd learn about the world in geography and surely history would be exciting. I liked numbers so maths would be good, and English meant books and reading. Drama! We were going to learn how to act. I had no idea what classical studies was, but it sounded good. PE would be fun, music amazing—perhaps I'd learn how to play the piano! As for art, the thought of entire blocks of time devoted to drawing and painting was incredible. Okay, maybe I was a swot.

I was so keen to learn and for this brief, sunshiny moment, I loved school. It was a love that wouldn't be long in the fading.

Chapter XXIV. High School

The bullying that I went through when I started high school was low-level, but it was constant. It was part of my everyday school experience to be pushed and shoved and be told *Get out of my way* by girls with sneers on their faces and hard glints in their eyes. The thing is, they didn't hurt me, not really. Not physically. They didn't mark me, didn't leave bruises. Not like the tiny girl in Maureen's class, who was made to crawl under all the desks when the teacher was out so that everyone could kick her as she went by on her hands and knees. All they did to me was push and push and push.

It didn't take me long to become disillusioned by some of my classes. The sewing part of home eccy was worse than I expected. While the boys sawed and hammered and cut metal, we were sent back to the 1950s to make a frill-edged apron with our name embroidered on the bib. I didn't get as far as the embroidery. The cooking classes weren't much better. We began by making tea and toast and built up to baking a thing. The thing was a whole cooking apple, peeled, cored, and wrapped in leaden pastry before being baked in the oven. It was quite something in its own way and I've never seen anything like it since.

Religious Education was compulsory but not taken seriously, not even by the school. In a campus containing upwards of 1,800 pupils, there was one RE teacher and she was older than Methuselah. With her tweed suits, thick-woollen tights, brown brogues and interesting features, she looked like a Cubist version of Margaret Rutherford's Miss Marple. She was permanently on the brink of a nervous breakdown and frequently teetered over the edge. In the two years I spent in her class, religion was never mentioned. Sometimes she gave us handouts with a Charlie Brown cartoon on them and maybe a word game, but mostly she spent her time trying to control the class. One day, there was uproar when a big dog started shagging a wee dog on the grassy slope outside the classroom and everyone rushed to the window to watch. There was another uproar when one of the boys unscrewed something on a radiator and the class was flooded. When we got too loud, a teacher came in from a neighbouring classroom to settle us down. No matter the teacher, they all wore the same weary expression. *Oh fuck, here we go again.*

One winter's day when I was shuffling down the icy hill to school, my feet clad in a pair of superbly unsuitable brown wedges, the bus from Glasgow pulled in just as I was going by the stop. A short play unfolded in front of me. The RE teacher got off, a look of terror in her eyes when she saw the untreated paths. Behind her, a geography teacher disembarked. When he saw the RE teacher clinging to the railing, a classic look of dismay came over his face as he realised that he'd have to help her. He offered his arm and she gratefully clung to it while he looked like he'd rather be facing a firing squad.

The RE teacher disappeared after second year and wasn't replaced. Instead, we had a series of random teachers. Except for the time we got the alcoholic history teacher, they mostly just let us get on with our homework. The alcoholic history teacher used the opportunity to express his views on why racially mixed marriages were a bad idea. He did nothing to enlighten me about religious matters, but he at least confirmed to me that teachers could be complete wankers.

The '70s was a turbulent decade with many strikes and protests, and my first year English teacher was mostly out of the class on union business. One day, she told us to take a book out of the cupboard to read until she got back. I found *Lord of the Flies* and was engrossed when she came bustling back and tore it out of my hands. *That's for third years.* But banning stuff always just makes it more desirable, so, after school, I went up to the library in the toonie and found a copy there.

If going to the toilets at primary school was hazardous, at high school it was truly grim. The toilets were in the basement and there was an old woman living there. I mean I know she didn't actually *live* there but that's what it seemed like. She had her own chair at the end of the sinks. I never knew why she was there or what her purpose was supposed to be but what she did was smoke and joke with the tough girls. There was always a used sanitary towel on the floor and, even if the mirrors weren't actually cracked, they gave the impression they ought to be.

I didn't like being pushed around by the tough girls but it was preferable to being groped when moving from class to class. A one-way system was in operation in the corridors but using the central staircase was chaotic and, if you were going from building to building, it couldn't be avoided. There was such a crush of people going up and down that it was impossible to turn around. It didn't help that we weren't given lockers, so everyone had to carry everything around all day long: schoolbag, PE kit, coats, jackets, jotters, books, packed lunch. Everything.

You were carried along with the flow of bodies and had to break out at the right floor. Teachers stood on the landings to make sure no-one was trampled to death, but they couldn't see into the throng. They couldn't see the hands that wormed their way between my thighs as I went upstairs. But still it happened. Not every day, but several times each week and sometimes several times in one day. The humiliation of being groped in a crowd, of feeling someone poking and prying at me, sent my face scarlet. It was even worse if I had my period. I was ashamed that they'd feel my pad and know. The embarrassment was excruciating.

I couldn't turn around, couldn't do anything except keep going while someone was assaulting me from below. Even if I could have turned around, drawing attention to what was happening would have only resulted in jibes and rumours and yet more shame heaped on me. My feelings of shame were sharpened by guilt. It was like the situation with *Uncle* Allastair. Why was this happening to me? What had I done to encourage it? Why couldn't I stop it? We lived in a culture of victim blaming, a culture I endorsed by blaming myself.

Chapter XXV. 🌍🌍 The Different World Next Door

The neighbours from Stornoway moved back there and a couple with a cat moved next door. My sister went to their door and asked if she could take the cat for a walk and the man ended up in our living room, drinking a can of Tenant's Lager with my dad while we watched *Chitty Chitty Bang Bang*. The new neighbours were getting divorced and didn't stay long and then we got more new neighbours.

Olivia was from Switzerland, Tarif from Iraq, and going into their house was like entering another world. It was a world I was besotted with to the point of making a pain in the arse of myself. Their house was identical in layout to ours but from the huge sandalwood candle on their coffee table and the sheepskin rug casually slung over the couch, to the stuffed leather camel ornaments from Iraq and the shelf of intriguing-looking books, it seemed so different, so utterly cool.

They became good friends with my parents. They socialised together and I spent a lot of time in their house. I listened, mind blown, when Tarif expressed concern about his friend Haq, who like Tarif, was a university lecturer but still lived in Iraq. When they talked on the phone, they had to communicate in code because the Iraqi government listened in, but Tarif was worried he hadn't heard from Haq in a while.

He did finally get in touch and I later met Haq when he brought his family over for a visit. They had a little boy and my dad took them for a day out to Blair Drummond Safari and Adventure Park. When the car broke down in the lion enclosure, they had to sit with the windows closed, waiting for the rangers to rescue them. Haq took the opportunity to smoke a large cigar. Later when the car was running and the cigar fumes cleared, my dad excitedly drew the little boy's attention to a camel. Haq drolly informed him, *These are like cows to us.*

Tarif told me what it was like to arrive in London as a student from Iraq who couldn't speak English and the confusion at breakfast in the refectory when he and other foreign students were faced with bowls of cornflakes and jugs of milk laid out on the tables. The bewildered students poured the milk into glasses and ate the cornflakes dry, the sound of their crunching like an army on the march.

Tarif showed me his diary, written in Arabic, and listened when I told him about ideas I had, seemingly just as fascinated in my ordinary life as I was by his more exciting one. They had two young sons and I loved staying overnight in their house. In the morning, we'd spend a long time at the breakfast table, eating continental cheese and talking about all manner of things. Olivia told me about her brother who was in a rock band in Switzerland and how he had a tank of piranhas in his home. It all seemed very sophisticated to me.

Tarif took me to see *Jaws* at the County, just the two of us, his treat. When he called in for me, I was standing on the top landing, my feet a little above his eyeline. He caught sight of my clumpy platform shoes. They weren't very platformy compared to the fashionable, giant blocks worn by tough girls, but they were enough to elicit a gasped, *My God,* from Tarif.

Tarif had one suit. He wore it for work and when he got home, he changed into pyjamas and a silk dressing gown with a paisley lining. He wore leather mules and liked to relax with a large whisky. He was amused by my liking of chemistry, surmising that I enjoyed how everything was ordered. He was right. I found it so exciting that everything that existed in the entire world was represented by the beautifully laid out letters and numbers on the periodic table of elements. He encouraged me to study physics, telling me it was an important subject, and it was because of Olivia that I chose German instead of Latin. Not that it amounted to much in the end.

When I was 16, I turned up steaming drunk at their house on Hogmanay[34]. It was a pretty daft thing to do, considering I knew my mum and dad were there and I could just have gone home with no-one any the wiser, but I was

---

[34] Hogmanay is the Scots word for New Year's Eve. Until recently, Hogmanay was a much bigger celebration than Christmas. I'd rather give Christmas the bye-bye to just have Hogmanay and New Year's.

stupid that way, always poking the bear. Olivia never batted an eyelid. She just made me coffee and asked whether I'd been drinking or smoking something. My parents were nowhere near as cool about it, though they saved their wrath three days before sitting me at the kitchen table for one of their talks.

In carefully modulated tones, they told me everything that was wrong with me and how disappointed they were and what a disgrace I was and how much I'd upset my mother. *You've upset your mother. You've upset your mother. You've upset your mother.* And because they were using these modulated tones, they called it a conversation and asked if I had anything to say. I said I was sorry, but it wasn't enough, so I said it again. *Sorry. Sorry. SORRY.* And I cried a wee bit to show that hurting them had hurt me and I promised not to do it again. *SORRYSORRYSORRYSORRYSORRYSORRY.*

It was Olivia and Tarif's house I went running to another New Year when my dad collapsed in the street and we thought he was having a heart attack. They'd moved by then and their house was closer to where he'd collapsed than ours. Olivia called for an ambulance. It came and it turned out that the only thing wrong with my dad was that he'd drunk too much. My mum was mortified, and later they gave me into trouble for getting other people involved, even though we thought at the time my dad was dying.

I tasted new and exciting foods at Olivia and Tarif's house: dates stuffed with almonds, olives, lime pickle, Bombay Mix, tiny Swiss biscuits. I began learning about spices. *Cilantro—you call it coriander*, Olivia said when I'd never heard of coriander and hadn't called it anything at all. I learned that garlic was more than a tool for keeping vampires at bay— it could also be eaten—and that cinnamon could be bought in sticks. Olive oil wasn't just for earache; it too could be eaten. It took me a while to get over that one.

They acted as though my contribution to our conversations meant something and Tarif especially encouraged me to expand on my thoughts. This was my first experience talking about abstract concepts beyond the scope of my small world. It was my first experience of being listened to and it was exciting to be heard.

Chapter XXVI.

Joined Up Writing

A bunch of us were standing in the corridor, waiting to get into class when Gerry approached me. Gerry was one of the tough boys. I don't know how or when he'd paid his dues, but no-one ever messed with him.

Is it true that you can do joined up writing?

I nodded.

Will you write a letter for me, from my maw to the school?

This was an interesting development. Turned out Gerry had been dogging it and needed a note to explain his absence. I knew I'd be in big trouble if I was caught, but that only added to the thrill and I had enough sense of self-preservation to realise that doing a good turn for a tough boy was a smart move. Also, I liked Gerry. He was tough, but he wasn't mean, at least not to me. Gerry produced an envelope and a sheet of paper he'd swiped from home and I leaned on the wall to write the letter. I asked him what he wanted to be wrong with him and he said *diarrhea*, which was a common excuse for being off school, as you could be off one day and turn up the next looking fine. I wasn't sure how to spell diarrhea and thought I was being pretty smart when I wrote explaining that he'd had an upset stomach. I signed it with a flourish and handed him the letter.

Over the next few months, I wrote Gerry another couple of letters and, when he asked me to do one for his pal, I back-sloped my writing to make it look different. I took pride in these letters but we didn't overdo it and we never got caught. It was after that first letter that my situation changed. Suddenly, I was protected.

Now that I was a friend of Gerry's, the tough girls stopped pushing me around. I don't know how it worked. I doubt Gerry had words with them; I guess they intuited the shift in landscape and adjusted their behaviour accordingly.

The funny thing was, not only did they stop pushing me around, they also kind of became my guardians. If any other tough girls had a go at me, they defended me and so, pretty soon, I wasn't being shoved around anymore. Plenty of other people were still getting a hard time, though. I saw it every day and never once did I intervene. Nobody ever did. There was no nobility. Nobody wanted to put themselves in the firing line.

When I was a little kid, you just went out and played and some other kid would come and play beside you and that was it, but here, in this mass of people, I was lost. I didn't have a clue how to make friends. Most of the teachers told us where to sit in their classes. The girls I was put beside spoke to me in class but if I said hello to them outside, they'd either sneer or look right through me. It fucked with my head but there was some relief for a while when the tough girls took me under their wing. As a bonus, it meant that if Maureen wasn't at school, I had other people to hang around with at break and lunchtime. That's how I found out about corky.

Every lunchtime, an ice-cream van parked on the hill behind the high school and ant trails of kids wandered up and down to spend their lunch money on the single fags the ice cream man kept on a shelf above the hatch. The tough girls bought a single each and challenged each other to a game of corky, which meant passing a cigarette back and forth until it was down to the filter. The winner was the person who managed to get the last tar-filled drag.

It wasn't that these girls became my friends, it was more like I was their pet swot. I knew I wasn't one of them but, as long as I wasn't being pushed around, I didn't care. But, while there were small improvements at school, home life was becoming more difficult.

You can talk to your mother about anything.

This was a claim—a boast—made frequently by my father. He liked the idea of it, viewing my mother as a giver of wisdom with me as the grateful receiver, but him liking the idea didn't make it true. Though words frequently cascaded from my mouth and sometimes my mother listened and sometimes she responded, I couldn't talk to her about anything, especially not about anything that mattered.

You can talk to your mother about anything.

I was too ashamed to tell her about the bullying and too embarrassed to talk about the groping and she had no idea how lonely I was. My loneliness felt shameful, as though I was letting her and my father down by not being pretty and popular.

You can talk to your mother about anything.

But I couldn't talk about how difficult I found it to make friends or how different I felt from the other girls. I hadn't yet grasped that I might be a bit weird or that being a bit weird was okay. However wild and crazy the '70s look in retrospect, the pressure to conform was immense and I was a long way off from embracing my weirdness. It wasn't something my parents would ever accept. They didn't just want me to be normal. They wanted me to be *their* definition of normal.

You can talk to your mother about anything.

But whenever I tried to tell her I was upset about something, she told me to pull myself together.

You can talk to your mother about anything.

But when I asked her about what sex was, she said, *These plants need watering*, and fussed over the Busy Lizzies. And when I asked about practical things like bills and paying rent and how it all worked, she said, *Mind your business.*

You can talk to your mother about anything.

But when I tried to tell her there was a boy at school I fancied, she scoffed and said, *Don't be so silly.*

You can talk to your mother about anything.

No, I couldn't. My mother knew I enjoyed reading but she never understood books were an integral part of my life. She thought that it was nice that I could draw but she wasn't interested in art. In years to come, I discovered that her feelings were not as ambivalent as I'd thought. What she really thought about art was that it did not matter. That it was a waste of time.

We had our shared family experience, but beyond the mother–daughter dynamic we had nothing in common. Even physically, we were worlds apart. My mother was a petite woman, 5'4", even her size 4 feet. There was nothing neat or trim about me. By the time I was 11, I was a head taller than her and my feet were two sizes bigger. Standing beside her, I felt huge and ungainly and, like an ugly stepsister, I could not squeeze my cumbersome feet into her tiny shoes.

My mother always considered her own mother to be selfish and vain. She was determined vanity would never take hold of me. It worked. I was the opposite of vain. On the rare occasions she did compliment me, it was through tight lips, as though she was trying to keep the words to herself.

You can talk to your mother about anything.

But...

Pull yourself together.

Don't be stupid.

What have you got to be upset about?

You don't know how lucky you are.

The message I received was that my feelings did not matter. I clowned around to cover up the pain I didn't feel and then, one day, I made a mean joke about someone and she laughed, so the next day I did it again. Mean jokes and acting daft became my currency at home, but all the while I was making sarcastic jokes, I felt I was swallowing myself whole.

The boys at school smirked when the girls filed out of the class to go to the science lecture theatre. They knew we were going for the period talk. The nurse was a sturdy, no-nonsense woman. She showed us diagrams of fallopian tubes and ovaries and held up sanitary towels and tampons. She had no time for euphemisms.

It's not your monthlies or the curse. You don't have the decorators in. It's your period. Say it. Say, Period, period, period.

And so we all chanted, *PERIOD, PERIOD, PERIOD.*

Again, the nurse said.

PERIOD, PERIOD, PERIOD.

Over and again, we chanted.

PERIOD, PERIOD, PERIOD.

PERIOD,

PERIOD,

PERIOD.

I was in geography when my period started. Last class of the day. I was scared to stand up in case I'd leave a puddle on the seat or there would be a stain on my skirt. I lingered, last to go, but I made it home without giving myself away. I locked myself in the bathroom and cried. Even although I knew about it in theory, *PERIOD, PERIOD, PERIOD*, it was still a shock to see blood coming out of my body and I didn't like the dull, leaden feeling in the pit of my stomach. I wanted a hug, reassurance. Instead, my mother snapped at me.

There's no point in crying. You'd better get used to it.

Sometimes, I felt as lonely at home as I did at school.

Chapter XXVII.  It's My Party

Auntie Margo's family had a cottage on Arran and, in June 1977, I was allowed to skip a week of school so we could all go on holiday with her and *Uncle* Allastair. I saw basking sharks from the ferry on the way over but, while I was watching them, I was thinking about what I was going to do if he came near me. They offered me a room of my own, but I said I wanted to be in with my sister. I wasn't going to take the chance of him doing anything to her. Every night, I went to bed tense, but he never came near me. Perhaps it was fear of being caught. Or maybe, at the age of 12, I was too old for his tastes.

I turned 13 that summer and, to mark the occasion of becoming a teenager, my parents decided to throw me a party. I was excited until I realised that—except for Maureen—I didn't have anyone to invite. It took most of the summer to scrape together a few guests and I ended up with seven boys and six girls. Of the boys, one was my cousin, so he didn't count, and another was the son of a friend of my dad's. He was from Cumbernauld but went to a different school. None of the other boys spoke to either of them.

There was Ryan, who'd marked me as a swot, but, over the year, we'd become friendly-ish. Another was Malky, who ripped me off a year or so down the line when I bought a Queen album from him, but, another couple of years after that, he'd help me get a job so that would square that off. Duncan was in most of my classes and sat in front of me in French, and then there was Gerry and his wee tough guy pal, Craig. Representing the female of the species was me, my pal Maureen, Boss Girl, and three of the Boss Girl's friends, two of whom I'd barely ever talked to. It had taken some effort plus the embarrassment of several direct knock-backs, but 12 guests was respectable, except the party was in a community hall near the Washing Well launderette and we were rattling around that big room like dried peas in a biscuit tin.

Being sophisticated teenagers, we did not play games but danced, the music provided by my dad's pal, Pat, who with set his music centre up in the corner. My parents, my real auntie and uncle, and the fake auntie and uncle, partied in another room and had a great night while Pat sat in the corner, playing records for us, his cigarette glowing as the light faded, witnessing all that went on.

My parents went all out with party food, our liquid refreshment coming by way of the Alpine man. Once a week, the big Alpine lorry rattled into our street, loaded with chunky glass bottles of exotically flavoured soft drinks—pineappleade, blackberryade, fluorescent-green limeade. There was always a bottle of Barr Lemonade kept in our house for my mother's whisky and, sometimes. my dad called me to fetch it for him in bed when he had a drouth on a Sunday morning, but bottles from the Alpine man were a rare treat. Except when it came to this party for my thirteenth birthday. My mum and dad catered for the dozens of friends they assumed I had. They didn't just buy bottles of Alpine, they bought crates of it. My sister and I were drinking it for weeks afterwards.

When it came time for food, I was disappointed when the girls and boys sat at separate tables, but I didn't have the brass neck to mix it up. After our dayglo limeade and pickled onion crisps, it was time for more dancing.

The boys must have been talking and decided that one of them had to dance with me, the birthday girl. Gerry drew the short straw, but the prospect was so bad, the rest of the boys had to get behind him and literally push him towards me. He looked like a mouse about to be swallowed whole by a python and I was equally stricken. A rictus smile was stamped on my face but I was dying of shame. I thought I must be the ugliest girl alive for him to be so terrified at dancing with me. As they propelled him towards me, I veered off. I was desperate to dance with a boy, but not that desperate.

I went and hid in the toilets to nurse my humiliation, but I couldn't stay in there all night. After a while, I swallowed it down and fixed the smile back on my face. I went through to the hall and danced with girls, pretending I didn't care, until the last song came on, a moony (slow dance).

I watched everyone pair off, trying not to cry as I wondered how they found it so easy. Even the Boss Girl's friend, the one who moaned a lot, was asked up. *What was wrong with me?* Finally, the son of my dad's friend asked me to dance. At least it wasn't my cousin. We shuffled around, as awkward and ungraceful as was possible for two people who weren't moving very much.

Chapter XXVIII. Tinned Snails

Our school rector, Mr Arnott, left and was replaced by a short, pugnacious character who wore a grey suit and a permanently angry expression. The house system and the school fair, indeed anything that engendered a sense of school community, was immediately axed.

There had been four houses in the school, each named after a freshwater loch—Achray, Morlich, Lomond, and Katrine. I was assigned to Achray. Everyone was encouraged to earn points for their house, mainly through sporting achievements, so I decided to have a crack at the swimming gala.

From the moment the Tryst Sports Centre opened in Cumbernauld in 1974, it was a big hit. During the summer, the queues for the swimming pool snaked out the door. I learned how to swim there when the primary school took us for lessons. I grasped the basics quite quickly but splattering through the water for 50 yards to get my Scottish Swimmer certificate was pretty much the pinnacle of my swimming career. My dad saw me in the pool once and got the bizarre notion that I was a marvellous swimmer.

Later he said to my mum, *You should have seen her powering through the water.* That's how he said it, *powering through the water.* He also said something about me having big shoulders and arms, the implication being that I was built like Johnny Weissmuller. I tried not to listen to that bit. It didn't matter that I wasn't great because there were so many kids in the pool that you couldn't go two strokes without banging into someone. It was basically people soup.

Buoyed up by my dad's praise, I convinced myself that I enjoyed swimming and was excited that the high school had its own pool. Much of my joy was extinguished by the horror of the communal changing room and the rest of it was shot to pieces the day my right tit decided to break free of my costume in front of every girl while I was strolling along the poolside. Before that happened, I swam in the gala.

Whatever my dad might have thought, I wasn't powering anywhere. Aside from not actually having the arms and shoulders of an Olympic swimming champion who played Tarzan, I had this thing about breathing. Whatever stroke I was meant to be doing, I kept my head above water the whole time. I decided to enter for the backstroke because it had the smallest number of entries and at least then I'd be able to breathe. On hearing this, the tough girls informed me that I was really stupid, as I'd be up against Linda Muirfield. Linda was an Amazonian girl who excelled at backstroke and won every swimming race she entered.

Linda terrorised me one freezing morning when she emerged from the fog and came charging towards me, big stick raised ready to strike. In her defence, we were supposed to be playing hockey at the time, a game as unfathomable to me as netball. I took one look at her and ran. In the gala, she duly powered through the pool and won the race, but I didn't come last, which was a win in my book.

With the arrival of the new rector, there were no more galas. Where Mr Arthur had talked to us of hope and aspiration, his successor thundered threats and told us how we would never amount to anything. He strode about the schoolgrounds with a snarl on his face and called us scum while his tall deputy loped miserably by his side. His words and actions suggested he thought us wild beasts to be cowed and controlled—rather than young people who should be educated and encouraged. He was a horrible, wee man. The very opposite of everything New Town represented. Into his school, I brought my Mucky Pup.

The Mucky Pup was a piece of brown plastic moulded to look like a convincing dog turd. I'd bought it at Tam Shepherds Trick Shop in Glasgow and I'd been having great fun with it at home, leaving it in increasingly absurd places and making my mum and dad and sister laugh. I showed it to Ryan and he suggested that I put it under a table at the front of the first class we had that day. I thought this was a great idea and we were all happy, buzzed up and waiting for the teacher to come in so that we could see his reaction. Unfortunately, our regular teacher—a person who might/probably would have seen the funny side—was off that day and instead in came this hulking brute of a maths teacher. He clocked the Mucky Pup the moment he walked in but said nothing. Anticipation turned to apprehension as I exchanged looks with Ryan. We spent the period doing our homework in oppressive silence. It was almost over when the teacher pointed at the plastic shit.

Who put that there?

Everyone knew it was me, but nobody said a word. The entire class sat in a silent ball of tension until the buzzer went and we were released. What I should have done was walk out of the room with everyone else. What I did was pick up my Mucky Pup. My world became a darker place as the teacher's shadow fell over me.

He took the plastic jobby from my hand and launched into a tirade about what a disgrace I was and how he was tempted to put it on a string and make me wear it around my neck for the rest of the day. He waved the turd in my face.

How would you like that? HOW WOULD YOU LIKE THAT?

In truth, I was not particularly bothered at the thought of wearing the Mucky Pup hanging from a string around my neck. I actually thought it might be quite funny to wear a plastic jobby necklace but, realising that this was not the response the angry man required, I shook my head.

No, sir.

What's your name? I'm going to write to your parents about your disgusting behaviour.

I wasn't so amused now. Throughout my comeuppance, he towered over me, never touching me, but getting right in my space, ranting in my face like a man possessed. Finally, he told me to go. I hesitated, waiting for him to return my Mucky Pup. Instead, he slipped it into his pocket and ordered me out.

Ryan and some of the other boys lingered in the corridor and witnessed the entire scene.

Why did you pick it up? Why didn't you just walk past it?

I shrugged, not answering. The truth was simply that it was mine and I wanted it back.

The angry man did not write to my parents but, all the same, I kept my head down whenever I passed him in case my face served as a reminder to spur him into action. Then I realised he was one of those teachers who never made eye contact with pupils. Instead, he kept his head high as he strode along the corridor, as though we were a stream of effluent passing beneath him and he was pretending we didn't exist.

My history teacher was a much friendlier man. He was a big, beefy sort with a classic '70s 'tache. In first year, he taught us about Mesopotamia. It was at this point that I lost all enthusiasm for history. I thought it would be exciting, when in fact it was so boring, it made geography seem interesting. In second year, we were taught about the Glasgow Tobacco Lords. These were men who made their fortunes trading tobacco in the 18th century and then made ostentatious displays of wealth by commissioning extravagant houses that can still be seen in Glasgow today. There's one on Queen Street that was originally built as a private mansion and now houses the Gallery of Modern Art.

Evocative street names such as Virginia Street and Jamaica Street echo that time and make it sound like a great adventure, glossing over the fact tobacco was grown by slaves. Our architectural legacy was built on their blood, but the Glasgow Slave Lords has quite a different ring to it.

One day, the history teacher came up behind me and decided that it was a good idea to tickle me. Even for the 1970s that was quite weird. I laughed involuntarily, squirming on my chair, my face beaming scarlet as his fingers wiggled between my arms and body. Meanwhile, knowing looks passed between Ryan and some of the other boys and, because I was laughing, it felt like it was my fault.

Mostly in school I just kind of sat there but, every now and again, I felt the need to make a complete arse of myself. I was into rockabilly and rock 'n' roll and it was a known thing that I liked Elvis. We were in history and our overly friendly regular teacher was off so one of the other history teachers was standing in. He was as bored as we were and so when

Ryan started egging me on to do an Elvis impersonation, the teacher sat back and let it happen. Ignoring the boring, wee voice in my head that told me not to do it, I stood up and swung my arm around while belting out "Heartbreak Hotel". Half the class cracked up. The other half were mortified on my behalf. The teacher, he just sat back and slowly shook his head.

Elvis made his presence felt again in my English class when Mrs B told us to write about a hobby we had.

Watching television isn't a hobby and you're not getting away with saying reading is your hobby. I want something more.

I stared at her in quiet horror, my mind a hazy shade of blank. The only things I did that could remotely be called hobbies were reading and watching telly.

Looking after my sister after school, it was *Wacky Races* with Penelope Pitstop and the Anthill Mob, Dick Dastardly and Muttley, *heeh-heeh-heeh-heeh-hee. Scooby Dooby Doo, where are you? Grange Hill.* Tucker Jenkins, Benny Green, a boy in my science class fancied Trisha Yates. *The Magic Roundabout.* Dougal the dog. *Calimero* the wee chick with an eggshell on his head. *It's an injustice, it is. The Wombles.* Orinoco. Great Uncle Bulgaria. Roobarb. *Top Cat. Close friends get to call him TC.* Benny the Ball, Choo-Choo, Brain. *What's up, Officer Dibble?*

Saturday morning before the programmes began on BBC1, the test card girl playing knots and crosses with the creepy toy clown, while, on BBC2, beardy men scribbled equations on *Open University.* Then it was *Bagpuss, Emily loves him. Multi-Coloured Swap Shop* had to do until *Tiswas* arrived. The Phantom Flan Flinger. Bob Carolgees singing, Houdi Elbow. *Joe 90* in a twirling onion. *Marine Boy.* Daffy Duck. Bugs Bunny. *This is the voice of the Mysterons.* Yosemite Sam. *One banana, two banana, three banana, four. Size of an elephant!* Foghorn Leghorn. *Get on board with the Double Deckers!*

Wile E. Coyote. ACME Corporation. *Barnaby the Bear's my name.* Saturday afternoon BBC2 Brian Cant and Floella Benjamin on *Play Away.*

The wrestling on *World of Sport* at my granny's. Giant Haystacks vs. Big Daddy. Having to be quiet while my dad checked his coupon. *Doctor Who.* Jon Pertwee. Tom Baker.

Cybermen. Daleks. Sunday afternoons *Glen Michael's Cartoon Cavalcade*. Paladin the magic lamp. Never enough of *Casper the Friendly Ghost*.

Summer holidays *Abbott and Costello* on Saturday mornings, *Robinson Crusoe* through the week. 5,000 episodes. Christmas Holidays Laurel and Hardy. *Poor little Laughing Gravy. Towed in a Hole. Sons of the Desert.* Sunday afternoon melodramas. *Why ask for the moon when we have the stars?* Johnny Weissmuller wrestling rubber crocodiles in *Tarzan* movies. *Daktari.* Clarence the cross-eyed lion. *Captain Pugwash* urban myth. There was no Master Bates or Seaman Staines and the young lad aboard was called Tom, not Roger the cabin boy. *Yabba dabba doo!*

I did not play sports or dance or collect anything. I didn't knit or crochet. I did not belong to any groups or clubs. Aside from minding my sister, watching telly and reading, the only thing I did with any regularity was wander around Woolco every Friday night with Maureen. We flicked through albums in the music department and then flicked through the poster carousel, neither of us with any money in our pockets. After, we'd stroll through the food section where, if the fancy took, you could buy a can of snails. Though I never mentioned it to Maureen because I didn't want to seem weird, the tinned snails were my favourite part of the shop. The can containing the snail meat sat at the bottom of a clear plastic tube, the upper part filled with obscenely large shells. Though I looked every week, I never once saw anyone buy a tin of snails.

Walking around a department store wasn't going to cut it as a hobby. The only other thing I could claim to have interest in was music and so I decided to write about Elvis. When I began my essay, I realised I didn't actually know anything about him. By this time, everyone else had their head down and the room was filled with the sound of scratching pens. We had no internet, Google was decades away, and half the class didn't have phones in their houses, let alone one you could walk around with. All I had to work with was what was in my head, and so, I began... *Elvis Presley was born in Hollywood.* It made sense. He was American, Hollywood was in

America and I was pretty sure he wasn't from New York, so he must be from Hollywood. There was a kind of logic to it.

We had to finish our essays as homework, and it was only when I read mine out to my mum and dad and they fell about laughing that I realised I had a disaster on my hands. I wasn't in the habit of reading my work to them but, because it was about Elvis, I thought they might like it.

So, where was he born?

Graceland.

It turned out that they didn't know any more than I did, so, knowing exactly zilch about my subject, I filled the required two pages with made-up information.

Once she'd marked our efforts, Mrs B was typically frank, her rant leaving us in no doubt of what she thought of us. Yes, us. As it turned out, hardly anyone in the entire class had a hobby beyond watching television. She said the best essay was written by a boy called Stevie. The entire class looked at him in surprise. One of Billy Blood's gang, Stevie looked a bit like the cartoon boy, Bod, and usually scored Es and Fs but it turned out that he wrote a beautiful essay about keeping pigeons. Well, who knew?

Stevie, who was one of Billy's thugs, sat with his hands clasped on the desk, looking humbly angelic as Mrs B heaped praise upon him and rained contempt on everyone else.

Fact: Elvis Aaron Presley was born on the 8th of January 1935 in Tupelo, Mississippi.

Chapter XXIX.

My Unfunny Valentine

The chairs in the drama class were arranged in a U-shape around the walls so the floor space was clear for all the performing we never did. We had a couple periods of drama a week but the teacher was often away on union business and so we were left to our own devices. When a new boy joined the class, Billy Blood asked him his name and the new boy said, *I'm Michael. I'm from Swindon.* We all fell about laughing at his English accent and he was asked to say it over and over. *I'm Michael. I'm from Swindon. I'm Michael. I'm from Swindon. I'm Michael. I'm from Swindon*, until the novelty wore off and we reverted to playing Moochy Silence.

The rules were simple. Someone (a boy) shouted *Moochy Silence!* Everyone had to be quiet. We all sat staring at each other, waiting for someone to make a sound. The first one who did was piled on and punched. When I say everyone, the girls all kept quiet and played the game but it was only boys who piled on and only boys who were punched. It was one of the few advantages of being a girl.

A variation of the game was Moochy Silence Stiff, which meant you couldn't make a sound or move. We'd all be sitting there like statues, nothing moving but our eyes as everyone kept a watch on each other, just waiting, waiting, waiting for the slightest sound, the smallest twitch.

There was another game that didn't have a name. It happened spontaneously. Someone made a low *whoa* that dragged out and everyone joined in, slowly getting louder and louder: *whoooooooOOOOAAAAAAAA* until it built into a great crescendo, at which point a teacher from another class opened the door and we immediately clammed up, creating absolute silence. The teacher gave us a hard stare then closed the door and we cracked up. By the time my sister was in high school, this had morphed into singing the *Dallas* theme tune, starting low and getting louder and louder.

Doo-do-doo-do-do-do-do-do-doo...

New boy Michael from Swindon played along with Billy, asking him to repeat his name and, when the fun was done, Billy let him alone. It was a different story when an American boy with a blond crewcut and glowing tan showed up in our English class.

This boy keyed up pretty easily and Mrs B, who was quite a nice teacher but who also shouted at pupils for the nothingest of reasons, no doubt had some insight into his backstory because she didn't say a word when he got frustrated and thumped his fists on his desk. And even although she'd have had plenty to say if any of the rest of us did it, she didn't say anything when he threw his head into the crook of his arm then laid across the desk to calm himself. He did this on several occasions and she always let it pass.

After some weeks, it was noted that the American boy missed the same period of English every week. The story went around that this was when he visited his psychiatrist in Stirling. I'd read about this kind of thing in books and seen it in films but never imagined I'd be in the same room as someone who had a psychiatrist. I felt quite envious. I thought it would be amazing to have someone in my life whose job was to listen to everything going on my head and help me sort it all out. But even though I was jealous of him having a psychiatrist, there was no way I wanted to be this kid, especially not when he became a person of interest to Billy Blood.

Billy bided his time until there inevitably came the day when Mrs B had to leave class. The door had barely closed behind her when Billy began practicing his dark arts. He sat right behind the American boy, which made his work easy. I sat on the back row on the other side of the class, so I couldn't hear his murmured words of torment, but Billy was right inside that boy's head like a kid whisperer. He knew what buttons to push and, after a few minutes, the boy erupted. Suddenly on his feet, he picked up his chair and threw it across the class. He pushed tables aside and flung jotters around before flinging himself against the wall. He leant there, face buried in the crook of his arm and began wailing. This terrible, anguished moan filled the classroom, and, when there was no more space for the moan, he sobbed, giving it everything he had. All the while this kid was breaking down, Billy was yukking it up with Stevie and the rest of his acolytes.

When Mrs B returned, the American kid ran out of the class. While most of us were sitting with our mouths agape, Billy Blood's wide grin gave him away. Looking fit to kill, Mrs B marched him out of the class. I never saw the American kid again but Billy didn't have to look far to find his next victim.

Simon was as pale as boiled cauliflower. Small and thin, his narrow face was framed by lank, dark hair. Word got out that Simon had a medical condition that meant he couldn't feel pain. Billy took it upon himself to test the story by kicking the shit out of Simon on a recurring basis. What made it ultrasick was that, as each kick and punch connected with Simon's slight frame, both of them laughed.

Cruelty was so common, so casually dispensed, that I was always wary of revealing myself. My thought process went along the lines of *Don't let them see they've hurt you or they'll hurt you more.* But if I was going to trust anyone, who better than my best friend, Maureen? I wanted to tell her I fancied a boy in some of my classes. It took me a while to get the words out, but, once I did, sharing was fun. It felt kind of sunshiny to have someone to confide in without fear of being mocked.

That Valentine's Day, I was delighted to get a card through my door from this boy. I told Maureen about the card on the way to school and, later in French, when Malky asked if anyone received a Valentine, I said that I had and told him who it was from. To my horror, he asked the boy in question. The boy denied it, his denial so vehement that it verged on insulting. I duly produced the card as evidence. Malky took one look and said, *That looks like Maureen McKay's writing.* Maureen had very distinctive handwriting that looked as though an inky spider had scurried across the page and, as soon as Malky said it, I knew he was right.

I wanted to die right there and then. I couldn't believe I'd been so stupid, firstly in confiding in my best friend, and, secondly, in being blinded to the truth by so much wanting the card to be from this boy.

Mrs Mack was standing close by. She witnessed the exchange and I could see that she had grasped the humiliating picture in full colour. Given that cruelty was the norm and that Malky wasn't known for having the milk of human kindness flowing through his veins, I prepared to be torn to shreds—but Malky blindsided me. When he saw my face after his revelation, he turned back to his desk and never mentioned it again. I put the card back in my bag for later destruction. Mrs Mack pretended she hadn't seen or heard anything, and nobody else said another thing about it, me included.

I was too hurt to confront Maureen. I'd be like a snail without a shell if I let her know how much she'd hurt. I especially didn't want to risk crying in front of her. I was bottling so much, I was scared to start in case I got locked into an eternal crying jag. And there was this: I was scared of losing my best—and only—friend. If I didn't have Maureen, I'd have to walk to school by myself. I'd cut a lonely figure during break and lunchtime. I wouldn't have anyone to wander around Woolco with. I had no people. I'd be on my own. So, I bottled this hurt along with the other hurts and buried it deep inside the sore place.

Chapter XXX. Pitched Battles

The 1970s is well-documented as a time of turbulence. Throughout the decade, there was large-scale industrial action as workers from gravediggers to bakers, teachers to train drivers, went on strike to fight for better pay and conditions. A strike by workers in Ford car factories in September 1978 sparked six months of bitter industrial actions over the coldest winter in a generation. During what became known as the Winter of Discontent, mountains of bin bags were piled high in streets across the country. London's Leicester Square was turned into an official rubbish dump while, in Cumbernauld, the grass verges of Central Way were heaped with uncollected waste. My father was an active union member and we gathered around the telly one night to watch him being interviewed on the news. He spoke well and was, as ever, on the side of the workers.

It was a time of mass demonstrations, marches, and protests, some of which ended in riots, notably in Lewisham in 1977 and in Southall in 1979. The Lewisham riot arose when anti-racist and anti-fascist groups took to the streets to protest against a National Front demonstration. When they violently clashed with the extreme right-wing group, the Met[35] waded into a fight that lasted several hours.

The Southall riot began when thousands of demonstrators gathered to protest a National Front meeting set up in an area with one of the largest Asian communities in the country. The riot became infamous for the death of Blair Peach, who was hit twice in the head by police truncheons then left unconscious in the street. Peach, who was a teacher for special needs children and an anti-racism activist, died from the injuries.

The riots, demonstrations, strikes and protests arose from people's desire to create a better society for themselves,

---

[35] The Metropolitan Police, responsible for policing Greater London.

their families, their friends and neighbours. They were fighting social injustice but, on the terraces and in the streets, football hooligans rioted for the sheer hell of it. While pioneers of the glam rock scene like David Bowie and Marc Bolan challenged cultural definitions of what it meant to be male, football hooligans reinforced stereotypes of toxic masculinity.

The 1970s saw the emergence in England of organised hooligan gangs known as firms, each firm associated with a specific football club. On the news, we saw shops local to football grounds boarding up their windows and pulling down their shutters before games. There were filmed reports of pitch invasions and gangs of aggressive males strutting through streets, chanting and clapping, jeering and sneering, making their presence felt. Clashes between rival firms were vicious, with weapons such as axes, meat cleavers, darts and knives recovered by the police. Stabbings and lootings and casual violence were rife.

In central Scotland, over 400 miles from London's Millwall Football Club, we were not unaffected by the images of raw aggression transmitted into our homes. I watched a boy in my year run along the corridor at full pelt, then leap up and slap an overhead beam while he yelled *Millwall!* He had a massive grin on his face and his friends were all laughing. It would have been a nothing kind of thing if it wasn't for the feverish excitement generated by football hooliganism.

In the following days, several pitched battles took place between boys from Greenfaulds and boys from Our Lady's High. They fought at lunchtimes on a grassy hill halfway between the two schools, the Greenfaulds mob running up, the Our Lady's mob running down, each out for their share of tribal belonging and gratuitous violence. Right in the middle of it all was Billy Blood and his acolytes.

I only witnessed the final battle. It wasn't like one of the after-school fights where the two protagonists changed their minds about having a go. These boys were committed to fighting. They laid into each other, fists pummelling torsos, knees connecting with faces.

A few minutes into the battle, the headmasters and deputies from the two schools turned up. The fighters fled the battlefield and that was the end of the pitched battles. The problem down south wasn't so easily eradicated. By the time football hooliganism peaked in the 1980s, it had spawned a designer, label-wearing sub-culture known as casuals.

Chapter XXXI. High Dusting

In the working-class tenements of Glasgow, cleanliness was a matter of pride. Any woman who didn't keep her doorstep clean was thought a slattern. My mother brought this matter of pride with her to Cumbernauld and nurtured it throughout her life. I'm tempted to say she turned housework into an art form, but the truth is that her loathing of dust became a tyranny we lived under.

All the dusting, vacuuming, polishing, washing, ironing, tidying, cleaning, scrubbing, wiping and drying left precious little time for anything else, and maybe that was the intention. Laundry was washed and spun in a twin tub, which was laborious work, but, even when we got an automatic washing machine, there was no release from the dictatorship of the laundry cycle. We always had to wait for the cycle to finish, for the washing to be hung out. Once dried, everything was ironed, including underpants and socks. These were my mother's standards. Anything less she regarded as slovenly.

Ajax to scour the bath, Pledge to polish the furniture. Fairy Liquid for the dishes. Brillo Pads for the pans. Windolene, bright and pink as the Calamine lotion used to soothe chicken pox, was smeared across glass then buffed away until nothing but sparkle remained.

My mother went out to work for the CDC, starting as a cleaner before becoming a landscape gardener, then came home to iron bedsheets and pillowcases. *Your mother never stops,* my father said, taking pride in her industriousness. She mentioned women at work talking about a daytime drama called *Rooms*, muttering that she couldn't understand how they had time to sit and watch TV during the day.

It wouldn't have killed us to have un-ironed vests. I want to go back in time and tell her to do something for herself. Climb a mountain, take up yoga, write a poem, run barefoot on the beach, join a choir, go out and meet a friend for coffee. Anything but this unnecessary toil.

One thing she did enjoy doing was baking. She excelled at making pastry. At Christmas, the shortcrust pastry for her mince pies was so light, it almost floated, but she never taught me how to bake. The kitchen was her domain and I don't think she could stand the thought of any mess I might make.

I was fascinated to go into other people's houses and see books and magazines and random stuff spread around the living room or in the corner: a pile of ironing heaped in a basket. Not that our house was minimalist. In fact, there were ornaments everywhere, polished and gleaming, but the detritus of daily life was constantly swept away.

The earliest ornaments I remember were glass swans filled with water that was coloured with special dissolving paper. One day you could have red swans, blue the next. Then there was her wooden animal phase. The crowning glory of her collection was an African bull elephant flanked by two giraffes. I was charged with dusting the living room when I got home from school, which included polishing the wooden animals with teak oil. I bestowed personalities upon them, making a game of it to distract myself from the futility of it all. One of the wooden gazelles was really mean.

I never saw the point of cleaning something that was already clean. After the wooden animals came fancy, ornamental jugs and delicate figurines of fine porcelain that had no personality at all. There was no escaping the purge of cleaning. Bleach down the toilet, Brasso for the knick-knacks. Even the bedroom I shared with my sister was not exempt. I regularly dusted my bookcase but, one day, I came home to find that my mother had cleared the shelves.

She removed every book she decided I had outgrown, including a weighty fairy tale she and my father gave me one Christmas. The dust cover had long since disintegrated, but the forest green, cloth-bound cover with its gold, embossed lettering was in perfect condition. This was a book I cherished. I started reading it the day I received it, sitting under the table, chewing on the toffees I always got in my stocking, and enjoyed it ever since. All the well-known tales by Grimm,

Anderson, and Perrault were represented, alongside more obscure stories, none of them sanitised. These were dark tales, full of wicked intention and gruesome detail. Eyes were pecked out and toes lopped off. Starvation was frequently at hand and death stalked every page.

The stories sparked my imagination and delighted my morbid curiosity, but it was the stunning illustrations that brought the book alive. They came in an array of styles: Some were loosely lined and exploding with colour, while others were life-like and fantastically detailed. I could see exactly how the sausage was attached to the woodcutter's nose and study the myriad snakes, frogs and lizards spewing from the spiteful stepsister's mouth. I could see how beautiful the princesses, and how ugly the witches. My favourite illustration was of a poor student who lived in an attic and had only books to warm and nourish him. The picture showed him sitting in his sparse room, gazing at an open book on the table before him. His face was lit up by a golden glow emitting from the pages and floating within that light was a world of knowledge.

Within its covers, my book held riches of words and images, but that was not all. It also had a flaw that annoyed then delighted me. Two blank pages, and then later in the book, another two blank pages. My annoyance arose from missing parts of those two stories, but, the longer I had the book and the more I read it, the more I looked forward to seeing these white pages. All that print, all those words and images and then... nothing. Blank pages that shouldn't have been there and only I knew about them.

Then the book was gone. Others had been cleared out, but that's the one I remember. That's the one that hurts. I was even a little bit heartbroken. I think perhaps the reason I remember the illustration of the student so well was because he was me. Books were my window into worlds beyond what I experienced. They were my joy. They were my escape.

The clearing out of my books was never discussed. I wasn't asked which should stay and which could go. I just came home and found them gone then I was told off for complaining when I should have been grateful. *It's only a book.*

And still the dusting went on.

Chapter XXXII.

Sticks & Stones

In the 1970s, we were more in touch with the seasons than people today. We could only get strawberries in the summer and even then they were an expensive treat. If you wanted to eat them any other time of year, you bought them tinned but they were expensive and tasted only of red mush. When I was small, my mother extracted whole strawberries from jars of Hartley's Jam and fed them to me in all their sweet, sugary glory.

In the late summer, I'd pick brambles[36], returning home with purple fingers and be told off for my similarly stained clothes. At Hallowe'en, we ate monkey nuts and sharp Cox's Pippin apples. Lettuce, tomatoes, the Orange Mivvi, and Jesus sandals only appeared in the summer months. In late spring, we gnawed on sticks of rhubarb, combatting the sour taste by dipping the long, red stalks into brown paper bags filled with sugar.

Many missiles were also seasonal. At high school in the weeks leading up to Bonfire Night, there was the constant threat of bangers[37] being thrown into crowds of milling kids. The potential to be maimed at any moment added an extra frisson to the everyday fear of physical and verbal assault.

During winter months, any delight at an overnight fall of snow was tempered by knowing that I'd have to traverse the snowball alley to get to school. Scores of schoolboys swarmed over the banks at the sides of the paths, hurling snowballs at hapless fools such as myself, and there was no avoiding it. The thick hide of my Gloverall[38] gave me some protection, but, even with the hood up, it afforded little in the way of facial protection.

---

[36] Blackberries
[37] Fireworks similar to US cherry bombs
[38] A duffel coat with extra seams to appear more fitted

A snowball that fell apart, showering its victim in flaky, white loveliness wasn't much of a wheeze, so they'd press the snow into compact orbs of ice that hurt like a bastard when they caught a cheek already chafed by chill winds. For added value, these ice balls contained sharp stones and jaggy grit. The tradition of shoving snow down the back of someone's collar was reserved for boy-on-boy tussles but not so when it came to summer fun.

In the 1970s, if you had told me that rose hips[39] could be transformed into tea, jelly or syrup, I'd have thought you insane. In my world, rose hips came in two forms: On the bush, they were part of the scenery. Off the bush, they were a torment from Hell we called itchy cubes. A well-aimed rose hip can sting as much as a small stone, but, when one is dropped down the neck of your T-shirt and smashed against your back, the tiny hairs on the seeds irritate the skin, resulting in tortuous itching. To play the game properly, *Itchy cube!* was yelled as the rose hip was crushed inside your top.

The only thing to do to get rid of the itch was change your clothes. If my mother was home, this entailed facing a barrage of questions about *What happened? Who did it?* and *What did you do to make them do it?* That bit of the game was best avoided. To be honest, the entire thing was best avoided. I only did it to someone once and that was the Boss Girl. When she did it to me, it was the funniest thing ever. At least it was to her and everyone watching. But when I retaliated, she cried, and nobody laughed. Suddenly, I was the big baddie. It was a lose-lose situation but more fun than when my erstwhile pal, Basher, pelted me with stones.

I was in my neighbour's porch, knocking on their door. They were out and I was about to go home when Basher happened by. He must have been walking around with pockets full of stones, hoping to chance upon a victim and here I was. He started chucking the stones at me. By this time, I was half a head taller than him, and, had fear not turned my bones to jelly, I could easily have barged past him. Instead, I pivoted this

---

[39] Red, round fruit accompanying various species of rose plants

way and that as he pelted stone after stone, snorting with laughter as I went *Aye-ya, aye-ya!* over and over.

To make matters worse, a girl who lived directly across the road had spotted the action and made no attempt to hide her gleeful laughter as she watched from her bedroom window. After what felt like an aeon of humiliation, Basher ran out of missiles and just kind of sauntered off while I fled home, thoroughly ashamed of my feartiness.

Spring, summer, autumn or winter, it was never not the season for being hit by something, and sometimes that something was a chair. One day it was a chair that was thrown from a terrace in school. One of its metal legs crash-landed on the skull of a boy I knew who was into Frank Zappa. He was carted off to hospital. We didn't really do sympathy in the 1970s and empathy was unheard of, so, when he returned several days later with a big, white bandage around his head, he was henceforth known as Pope Penis the First.

Chapter XXXIII.

There's A Punk In The Playground

Most days I ended up walking into school behind this older boy who was a fan of Clint Eastwood. I knew he was a fan because he wore a denim jacket with the spaghetti western star's face printed on the back of it and **CLINT** embroidered across the shoulders. Fair enough, except the *L* and the *I* were too close for comfort so basically this dude was walking around with **CUNT** embroidered on his back. I don't know why he didn't get his head kicked in every day.

You saw these little signs of individuality splattered around the place but, with the arrival of punk on the scene, it all changed up a gear.

There were rules about music. If you liked rock 'n' roll or rockabilly, you weren't allowed to like punk. If you liked punk, you weren't allowed to like heavy metal or disco. If you liked disco, you hated punk. It was very tribal that way. It was also a slow burn, or at least it was in Cumbernauld. People got into the music early on but you didn't suddenly see kids strutting around in bondage trousers and mohair jumpers. It was more subtle than that. Mostly it was badges. We were all still wearing flares because that was the only trousers you could buy, but people were also wearing a Buzzcocks or a Stiff Little Fingers badge.

The first punk to turn up at school was in the year above me. Somebody said, *There's a punk in the playground*, and we all rushed to the classroom window to look. He was wearing black drainpipes, a white *Sid Vicious Is Innocent* T and his blond hair was all spiked up. It was so fucking exciting.

The second manifestation was at the Mungo, the weekly Thursday disco at the church hall. The DJ put on Kate Bush singing "Wuthering Heights" and we all gathered in a circle around this wee punk guy with spiky hair, watching as he did a weird flinging-about dance, spasms running through his skinny frame in pulse with the music. He was magic. I wanted to be like him. I wanted to hurl myself around like that and not give a fuck what anyone thought.

Although I liked the DIY ethos of punk, my own efforts were pretty pathetic and my lack of sewing skills did me no favours. When I tried to convert my flared jeans into drainpipes, I ended up with a big lump of material inside both knees. I still wore them. I didn't have many alternatives.

My efforts continued when I got a ticket to see The Stranglers at the Glasgow Apollo. I wanted to look like a punk but had limited resources. I hit on the brilliant idea of using my mum's red food colouring to paint around my eyes and used a little sable brush to paint it on the lower rim. It looked pretty freaky, but also pretty good and then I blinked. My eyeballs turned bright red. *COOL!* Then I blinked another couple of times and the colour washed away so I ended up going to the gig looking every bit as ordinary as I did at school, and, to be honest, about 80% of the rest of the audience were the same.

In the year 1979, there arose a new tribe. The bands Secret Affair and The Jam were in the charts and *Quadrophenia* was on at the pictures. *We are the mods, we are the mods, we are, we are, we are the mods.* And lo! The school corridors were awash with green parkas.

Chapter XXXIV.

Bonar Bridge

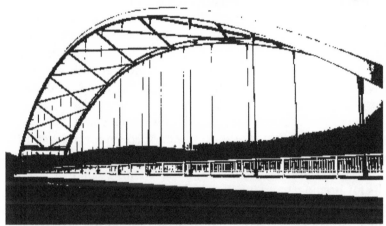

For our 1978 summer holiday, we went back to the Highlands to spend two weeks in Bonar Bridge. The drive was pretty much a repeat of our journey to Helmsdale a few years earlier. That's to say, Mum sat in the front *ooh*ing and *aah*ing at the scenery—*Look, mountains. Look, more mountains*—while my dad drove and my sister and I sat in the back, throwing up into poly bags.

Our suitcases—big, red cardboard affairs bought for our Isle of Man holiday—were tied to the roof of the car. On the way, my parents commented on the other cars with cases tied to the roofs of their cars, wondering why everyone had wrapped theirs in plastic. We discovered why when we opened them in our holiday cottage. Every flying thing we'd passed smaller than a sparrow was now trapped in the layers between our socks and pants and holiday Ts. The sight of our clothes filled with squirming insects sent my sister and I screaming from the room.

Our home for the fortnight was an old, ivy-clad cottage on the main street. The water in the cottage was peaty[40], a new

---

[40] Peat resembles soil, formed by partially decomposed vegetation. Peat bogs are common throughout the Highlands to be cut and dried in the

concept to me, and I freaked out when I ran a bath. I half-expected trout to come splurging out of the tap and I wasn't keen on washing in what looked like puddle water. On the positive side, there was an open fire and, while foraging for wood in the forest with my dad, I found a small rabbit. The fact it was dying from myxomatosis did not detract from the magic.

My dad put it in a box and took it back so my sister and I could have a pet for the holidays. Ignoring the pus running from its eyes, we *ooh*ed and *aah*ed over how cute it was and called it Bod. Bod ignored our offerings of carrot bits and, one morning, we awoke to find him gone, my father having released him back into the wild before he could die and unleash his fleas onto us. We were heartbroken for at least 10 minutes.

Our self-catering holiday meant eating a lot of filled rolls for breakfast and lunch, which was very good, and tinned ham for dinner, which wasn't. The jelly coating the ham brought my sensory issues storming to the fore and I spent forever and a bit of the following morning trying to scrape away every trace of it before picking at bits of pink meat. My sister wasn't much more inclined to tuck in and it drove my dad insane. He'd lose his temper, we'd end up in tears, and the next time we were given tinned ham for tea, we'd go through it all again.

In the evenings, my mum and dad went to the pub a few doors down, leaving my sister and me with some sweets for company. This suited me fine as I had a stack of holiday reading and was perfectly content to sit by the fire, burning the logs we'd stolen from the forest and getting stuck into James Herbert while my sister played with toys. I read *The Fog*, which includes the memorable scene where a PE teacher gets his throbbing member lopped off by one of his pupils. I was careful not to leave the book lying around in case my dad picked it up and had another freak out at what I was reading.

In the mornings, my mum had the radio on while she made up the picnic we would eat sitting in the rain. "Like

---

summer for use as fuel over the winter. Water running through peat is brownish in appearance.

Clockwork" by The Boomtown Rats came on and I leapt to my feet and did this jerky dance. Many years later, my sister told me it was one of the coolest things she'd ever seen. She was only nine at the time and didn't know any better.

I liked The Boomtown Rats. I had a few of their singles and enjoyed watching them on *Top of the Pops*, mainly because Johnny Fingers wore pyjamas while he pretended to play the piano, which was crazy stuff at the time. The following year, I read in the papers about a schoolgirl in California who shot her classmates and, when asked why, she said, *I don't like Mondays.*

It was a story that stayed with me and when The Boomtown Rats released a single called "I Don't Like Mondays," I knew it was about that incident. The record was a big hit and went to number one in the charts, and then I heard Bob Geldof on the radio, saying that the kids buying it didn't even know what it was about. There was something about the way he said it that made me think he thought I was stupid for buying his record. It put me right off him and I never bought anything by him again.

During our holiday, we went on a day trip to the Falls of Shin. This was long before there was a visitor centre owned by Mohammed Al-Fayed, owner of Harrod's and father of Dodi, lover of Princess Diana. There wasn't a proper path down to the river. People just made their way through the trees and stood on rocks at the side of the surging water, waiting for salmon to leap and occasionally land at their feet. The big fish thrashed around on the rocks for a few seconds before plunging back into the water and leaping up the waterfall, accompanied by a lot of *ooh*ing and *aah*ing.

My dad's pal and his family were on holiday in a house in Lossiemouth, which was only a gazillion miles away, so we went over and stayed with them a few days. This was the pal whose son had come to my thirteenth birthday. He had a sister called Jean, who was a couple years older than me and therefore sophisticated in the ways of the world. I went swimming in the sea with her. This was before swimming outdoors was called *wild* swimming, which sounds much more adventurous. We just called it swimming. After, we wandered around town, talking about music and looking for boys to ogle.

We stayed over so our parents could party and I slept in Jean's room with her, which was brilliant because she shared her wisdom with me, explaining what wanking meant and telling me lots of jokes about nuns and periods. Armed with this knowledge, I was all set for going back to school.

Chapter XXXV. Third Year

Third year at high school was the pits. I was trapped in a personal hell house of raging hormones, rampaging emotions, constant confusion, and silent screams. In my first two years at high school, I had gone from being pushed around and picked upon to some level of being accepted. There were people I could hang around with at break and lunchtime and, if I didn't exactly fit in, I was not entirely cast out. I'd found my place at the edge. It wasn't always comfortable, but it was mine. And then I made my subject choices and the tough girls who had protected and semi-accepted me were now in different classes, the school so large that I barely caught sight of them again. I had a new set of teachers and people in classes. Some of them eventually became friends, but not this year. This year, I was on my own.

The Apples, or a subset of them, were in many of my classes. I was an awkward dollop with chunky thighs, thick calves, and a chest so ample, it verged on vulgar. My nose seemed to be permanently running and I had greasy hair that was also frizzy. There was always a plook[41] somewhere on my face—a face that flamed at the slightest provocation. Worst of all, I was utterly clueless about who I was or where I belonged. Just about the only thing I did know about myself was that I wasn't an Apple.

The Apples were slender, petite girls. Wherever they gathered, it was as though a beautiful spring day had blossomed in a dismal corner of the school. They glided around in soft focus, tossing their glossy locks like models in a shampoo advert. They exuded confidence and seemed assured both of themselves and their place in the world. Their name arose from the way they displayed their healthy eating choices, hand raised to shoulder as though balancing a tray of drinks like a waitress in an American film, elbow to the side, wrist at

---

[41] plook: spot; blemish; pimple.

right angles, and the fruit, with one immaculate bite taken from it, held like an offering to the goddesses of popularity.

Everyone adored the Apples. The teachers liked them, boys fancied them, other girls fluttered around them, bathing in their reflected wonderfulness. Everyone except me.

Even although I wanted to be pretty and petite and popular with shiny, shiny hair, my dislike of them was not driven by envy. The barely noticed me, but I could see them and I didn't like what I saw. When they noticed me at all, their barbwire comments were sheathed in silky smiles. *What a shame you've spoiled that nice dress by wearing it with those baseball boots.* The tough girls were at least more honest.

There were 20 pupils in my new physics class, three of them girls. One me, two Apples. The seats were set out in three rows, with the girls grouped at the front. When the teacher left the room, which he often did as he was the Depute Head and had more important business to attend than teaching us physics, the Apples spoke to each other. The one beside me turned her back towards me and put her elbow across her table so that I was entirely blocked from conversation. They acted as though I did not exist and they did this in every single physics class for the next two years.

With their tinkling laughter and lovely demeanour, these were the kind of girls my parents wanted me to emulate, but I thought they were horrible. I may have been confused about who I was but I knew that I didn't want to be like them.

By the following year, the boys would turn human and we would speak to each other, but third year physics was a very lonely place. My new French class wasn't much better. The teacher told us we were terrible at French because we knew nothing about English grammar. The girl I sat beside spoke to me in class but ignored me outside. A neighbouring boy was enraged by my presence.

You're so ugly, no-one will ever want to get you pregnant.

There was some relief in Mr Tulloch's chemistry class. Despite getting into a stupid argument with him about wanting to keep my coat on in class, he didn't hold a grudge. He was one of the good guys. He was rarely out of the room and kept everything rattling along, and, best of all, he said things like *Californium is a ridiculous name for an element.*

English, a subject I'd enjoyed until now, was ruined. I was surrounded by Apples and my new teacher hated me. There was little opportunity for creative writing in her class. When we got the chance and I handed in a story about a man killed by a thing lurking in the sewers, she did not mark it. One day, she came in with her top blouse buttons undone, her bra and cleavage on show. I was embarrassed for her but since she ignored me whenever I put my hand up, I didn't bother trying. One of her pet Apples should have told her but they didn't and she spent the lesson with her quivering tits on display. My entire year in her class was made doubly miserable when she marked me down from an A to a B. My misery wasn't just churlishness on my part. The following year, in my English O'Grade[42] exam, I got one of the highest marks in Scotland.

Maureen wasn't in any of my classes, but I hung around with her at break and lunchtime, and, when she wasn't at school, I stood in the same spot by myself. An older girl had a spot nearby. She was always by herself. When I was also alone, the two of us looked at each other. We dressed differently and had different builds and colouring and she wore specs and I didn't, but it was like looking in a mirror and seeing my outsider status staring back.

This girl was awkward and weird and clearly had no friends. She was just like me and I hated her for it. I didn't really hate her, I just didn't want to be like her. One day, when Maureen was there and I was feeling bold, I spoke to the other girl. Not much, nothing nasty, just a couple of words in passing, one human being reaching out to another. I was spotted by Maureen's big sister, a tough girl with a gang of intimidating friends. Later, at their house, she dug me up about it. *What were you speaking to her for?* It was too complicated to explain

---

[42] O' Grades were the qualifications awarded following exams at the end of secondary school, O standing for Ordinary. These were our first exams that led to a qualification. We were judged purely on exam performance, no account taken of achievement throughout the year.

and so I shrugged and wondered if people were slagged off for speaking to me.

I watched *Rebel Without a Cause* on the telly and—aside from falling wildly in love with James Dean—I was wild about the film. There's a bit in it when Jim Stark says, *If I just had one day when I didn't have to be all confused and I didn't have to feel that I was ashamed of everything. If I felt that I belonged someplace... You know?*

It summed up everything I felt about myself. When people said to me, *Just be yourself*, I didn't understand what they meant. I had an internal monologue that was witty and full of sharp observation, but my awkwardness mangled the words on my tongue so that I felt lumpen and inarticulate. I had a rage growing inside me, but I hadn't yet worked out why I was so angry. I was shy but sought validation by showing off in ridiculous ways and getting into arguments with my parents and teachers that I could never win.

On one occasion, I locked myself into a staring match with a senior member of the teaching staff when he was berating the class. It went on and on, both of us unblinking. My eyes were burning but I wouldn't give in. I knew I could beat him and I could tell that he knew it too. Tension mounted in the room, discomfiting my classmates so that instead of egging me on, they told to stop. But I knew I could win. And then I realised there was no winning. This man could not afford to lose face. If I beat him, then, one way or another, he would have his pound of flesh and so I dropped my gaze and let him have his victory.

Despite having some decent teachers like Mr Tulloch, the only bright spot in my timetable was art. I loved drawing. It absorbed me. The concentration required blocked out all the anger and loneliness. I liked being good at it and wanted to be better. Being good at drawing marked me out in a positive way. It made me feel special and art was a good place to be, especially in third year when I moved into Mrs Muir's class.

Marianne Mitchel was the head of the art department when Greenfaulds High School opened in 1971, and she wanted to create something special. She believed that art was everything. *It opens our eyes; it reflects every part of our lives from the soap powder packet we choose to the houses we live in.*

She handpicked her staff, nine of them, including my old registration teacher, Mr David, and one of my previous art teachers, Archie Forrest, a painter and sculptor who was featured in the BBC arts documentary series, *Omnibus.*

Mrs Muir was a slender, elegant woman who wore her dark hair in a sleek bob. She wore black skirt-suits with white shirts, evoking the style of Chanel. She shared a large, brightly lit corner classroom with Mr MacRae, who was as passionate about art and the teaching of it. They synced perfectly, creating a brilliant vibe in the classroom. These were teachers I did not want to let down. I wanted to learn from them and impress them. When I heard Mrs Muir saying, *Lorraine is one of my girls*, I knew I had found my place.

Chapter XXXVI. ★ Legend

From the moment the first film was screened in the Empire Palace Theatre in Edinburgh in April 1896, the people of Scotland embraced going to the pictures. By the 1930s, Glasgow could seat more than 175,000 people in over 110 cinemas, which was more cinemas per head than any other city in the world, though it would soon be overtaken by another Scottish city, Dundee.

In the 1950s, the average person in Scotland was going to the pictures 36 times a year. If that person lived in Govan, they had nine cinemas to choose from without leaving the neighbourhood, but television was about to come of age, and, during the 1960s, half of Britain's cinemas closed. Perhaps this is why a cinema was not among the amenities housed in Cumbernauld's town centre when it opened in 1967.

Though cinema-going numbers were falling, going to the pictures was still a regular pastime for many. I don't recall my first cinema trip when my mum took me to see *The Jungle Book* in 1968 but I remember many visits throughout the years, including several to the Lyceum in Govan with my dad and cousin. But whether it was *Chitty Chitty Bang Bang* at the Lyceum or *Bambi* in one of the city centre cinemas, going to the pictures meant going to Glasgow. The only exception to this was when Uncle Bob put on a showing of *Planet of the Apes* in town hall one night. I regularly went to Uncle Bob's Saturday morning shows, but this was a new experience.

For a start, the audience was almost all adults. Later, when my mum gave my dad into trouble for taking me to see it, he said, *I thought it was a film about monkeys.* My dad covered my eyes when Charlton Heston's bare bum appeared onscreen, but it wasn't the sight of buttocks that gave me the screaming ab-dabs in the weeks to come. I got daymares rather than nightmares and started freaking out when I was in the bath, screaming, *The apes have stolen my clothes!* The trauma was a small price to pay. I loved that film.

Uncle Bob's Saturday morning film shows were great, but it wasn't the same as going to a real cinema with flip-down red velvet seats and usherettes with their torches and smart uniforms and the glamourous foyers and the anticipation when the lights went down. There was nothing about going to the cinema that I didn't like and so, when the County cinema opened in Cumbernauld in 1978, I was beside myself with joy at being able to walk there from my house.

Squatting in the bowels of the town centre, the County looked every bit the second thought that it was. The only reason it was there was because the County Bingo Clubs chain could only get planning permission for their bingo hall if they agreed to build a cinema next door. It was not a project conceived out of love and the minimum of effort was put into its creation. The completed cinema had the same cement waffle roof as the carpark so it looked as if all they'd done was box off a few parking bays then chuck in a screen and seats. 350 seats to be precise, in a single block.

The County was a soulless, utilitarian void but I loved it. Strangely, despite the bingo people's lack of enthusiasm for the cinema, they went to the lengths of employing a commissionaire. With his resplendent burgundy coat, shiny gold buttons and peaked cap, he would have looked perfect in the foyer of an art deco picture house but was slightly out of kilter in this chilly, concrete vault.

From the moment the County opened its doors in 1978, I went as often as I could and watched everything and anything from *Star Wars* and *The Buddy Holly Story* to *The Incredible Melting Man* on a double-bill with *The Savage Bees*, and I went to see *Grease* twice.

Wearing the green eyeshadow I'd gotten free with *Jackie* magazine years before, I blagged my way into X-rated films like *Carrie* and the mind-blowing double-bill of *Scum* and *Quadrophenia*. I was challenged a couple times but, while I was lacking confidence elsewhere, nothing was stopping me getting in to see George Romero's *Dawn of the Dead*.

No doubt it was my support that kept the County going the few years it was open, for, not long after I left, it was converted into a dining and bar area for the bingo hall.

Around the same time that I started going to the County, I discovered Cumbernauld's Cottage Theatre. This was my first experience of live theatre that wasn't pantomime. My father's union activities meant that political issues were always rumbling on in the background at home, but my own political consciousness was awakened by watching plays written by John McGrath for 7:84, the theatre group he founded. The name was based on a statistic stating that 7% of the population owned 84% of the country's wealth.

Hearing Scottish voices on the stage was one thing. Hearing them on the telly was something else altogether and it was rarer still to see Scottish working-class lives portrayed. No wonder there was such excitement in 1979 when *Just a Boy's Game* aired as part of the Play for Today series on BBC1.

Written by Peter MacDougall, who was born in Greenock, *Just a Boy's Game* told the story of Jake McQuillan, who aspired to the title of Greenock's hardest man. McQuillan was played by Frankie Miller, a brilliant soul singer from Bridgeton in Glasgow, where my grandad grew up.

It was a violent film, set against a background of shipyards and pubs, grim estates and hard drinking, but elevated by its rich, raw language and brutal humour. Though the setting wasn't our environment, we were all too familiar with the notion of the hardest boy in class, the central storyline resonated.

The day after it was shown, the school corridors echoed with guttural impersonations of McQuillan's immortal line, announcing it was time to settle the score: *McCafferty, your tea's oot.*

Similar joy was evoked a couple years earlier when *Roots*, an American slave drama based on the best-selling book by Alex Haley aired. As we only had three channels to choose from, everyone was watching it. Soon after, a boy at school was getting the belt and, when the teacher whacked the strap across his hand, he yelled out, *My name is Kunta Kinte!*

Absolute legend.

Chapter XXXVII. ☺ Before It Was Miles Better

In the 1980s, there was a campaign to promote Glasgow as a tourist and business destination. The tagline was *Glasgow's Miles Better*, accompanied by a Mr Happy logo. Before it was miles better, half-demolished tenements surrounded by rubble were strewn throughout the city. Solitary stripped walls stood lonely in the distance and broken pavements went on for miles. Where there had been life, there now grew only dust and litter and the mankiest of weeds.

Tenements were deconstructed slice by slice, creating gable ends that exposed what had recently been the privacy of family homes. These lives were displayed in patchworks of wallpaper four stories high. Lines horizontal and vertical marked the passing of walls and ceilings and floors. Doors and fireplaces lingered for as long as they had walls to cling. Shadows marked where mirrors and pictures used to hang.

It was a decade before the city's Garden Festival and accolades that followed, and Glasgow was still a gritty place. Forlorn scabs of wastelands, bordered by broken-windowed buildings, pocked the city. Litter swirled in alleys and children played in the rubbish-strewn backcourts of soot-shrouded tenements that would soon become patchworks of wallpaper four stories high.

Meanwhile, in Cumbernauld when I was walking from school, a boy ran up from behind and jammed his fingers between my legs. He was egged on by others who laughed at my scarlet face. For a few weeks or more, this happened most days. They were nice boys from decent homes. That they were younger than me increased my humiliation. I told no-one, and, if I had, would anyone have listened?

We left the city for a new town, a future, but we had internal wastelands and broken-windowed souls to contend with. We should have been better, miles better than this.

They should have been better.

Chapter XXXVIII. All Kinds Of Music

My fifteenth birthday fell on a skint[43] day so I didn't get a present from my parents until Mum got paid a few days later. She gave me some money so I went clothes shopping by myself in the toonie. I wanted to dress differently so I went to Woolco to try on a plain brown skirt and a dowdy cream shirt. They fit so I bought them then felt depressed and frustrated when I took them home.

My maths teacher, Mr Campbell, was always dressed in sharp three-piece suits. He had dark hair and the same trimmed beard as the Master in *Dr Who*, which gave him a slightly sinister air. He had great presence and addressed everyone formally, using their first and second names. Another maths teachers was renowned for throwing blackboard dusters at pupil's heads. You got the impression this behaviour was beneath Mr Campbell, that if he ever stooped so low, he'd treat himself to one of his own withering looks.

I sat in the corner beside the window and Ryan was at the desk in front of me. We were working on three dimensions and I told Ryan that I knew what the fourth dimension was. He gave me a sceptical look. *What it is then?* Triumphantly, I told him the fourth dimension was time. He thought about it a moment before acknowledging my genius. Genius I gleaned from the pulp comics I read. I would read anything I could get my hands on and recently came across *Papillon* by Henri Charrière. It was the first time I'd heard about lepers since saving up five-pence pieces for them in the Campaigners club.

I also sat at the back of my English class and, as in maths, Ryan sat in front of me. We were all trying to define ourselves and musical affiliation was a succinct way of stating tribal allegiance, but the lines were rigid. If you were into punk, you weren't allowed to like rockabilly. Mods sneered at rockers and the disco fans... Well, I don't really know about

---

[43] skint: lacking money; financially embarrassed.

them. Ryan was a head banger, meaning he was into heavy metal. One day in English, he turned around and sneered at me. *You like all kinds of music, don't you?*

I remember staring at him a long time while I weighed up the accusation. Not long after Sid Vicious died, I went to the Glasgow Apollo to see Bill Haley & His Comets. There was a teddy boy revival going on and I was a drab, wee sparrow agog at the peacocks in the queue. Suited up in velvet-collared drape jackets in solid blocks of blue, green and pink, they wore ankle-skimming drainpipes and brothel creepers, the quiffs of their DA (duck's arse) hairdos gleaming under streetlights. The Glasgow polis[44] were keeping a wary eye on the queue and there was a moment of excitement when a group of punks slouched by and the factions heckled each other. One of the policemen addressed the queue: *They're better behaved than you lot.* This didn't do much for the image of the punks but we were delighted and jeered in response.

Haley's "Rock Around the Clock" was a massive hit in 1955, when it was used as the theme tune for *Blackboard Jungle*, a film starring Glenn Ford as the teacher of a classroom of teenage delinquents. Dad told me when he went to see it, everyone went crazy when the music started. They'd never heard anything like it and were wild for it, dancing in the aisles and smashing up seats. I don't recall any smashed-up seats in the Apollo when I went, but there was plenty of dancing and good fun, even if Haley never looked like a rock 'n' roll rebel.

In the '20s, Glasgow had more dance halls than Britain. Though the number declined by the time my parents were courting, dancing was still a major part of the culture. They went dancing at the Dennistoun Palais, my father with his Tony Curtis hair and my mother in a pencil skirt and heels. The Palais was the biggest venue in the city with a capacity of 1,800. When I was living in Dennistoun, it had long since been converted into a depressing supermarket, the kind that looks mopped with dirty water, but, in the '50s, it was full of young people dancing and looking for a lumber[45].

---

[44] Glaswegian for police, pronounced *po-liss*.
[45] Lumber: to make a romantic or sexual connection with someone.

In February 1960, my parents went to a Gene Vincent–Eddie Cochran double-bill at the Glasgow Empire. Cochran, whose hits "Somethin' Else" and "C'Mon Everybody" were covered by Sid Vicious, died a few months later in a traffic accident at the age of 21. My parents were married that June so their honeymoon was a return trip for the Cochran tribute show starring Billy Fury, Joe Brown and Georgie Fame.

My parents liked music, but, for my dad, it was never-mind-the-quality, feel-the-width. When "Suicide Is Painless", the *M*A*S*H* theme, hit the charts, he went to buy it in Woolco, but instead of coming home with the 99p single, he returned with four *Top of the Pops*, as they were a bargain at four for a pound. These albums featured the latest hits but instead of the original artists, they used un-named session musicians. For added appeal, the covers featured pouting women.

My parents' record collection wasn't vast and, what music they did have, was played on a radiogram. This was the size of a small sideboard, split into three sections. One end housed the mono record player, then there was a giant radio, plus a cupboard to store vinyl. They eventually traded this in for an enormous record player and tape deck with stereo speakers that sat on the display unit in the living room.

As I stared at Ryan, I thought about how I'd gone to see The Stranglers and Roxy Music. I thought about the music I listened to—Bowie, Queen, The Jam, Talking Heads, John Lennon, Adam and the Ants, The Beatles, Elvis Costello, Bob Marley, George Harrison, and The Specials. I couldn't deny his accusation. After my carry on with Elvis impressions, everyone knew I liked rock 'n' roll and was now into mod music and had a green onion painted on my jeans in honour of Booker T. and the M.G.'s. The cheek of me.

A long silence spun out between us as I looked the air guitar-playing AC/DC fan in the eye. Then I said, *Yes, I do. I like all kinds of music.* Ryan stared back, letting the information sink in and then he shrugged. *Oh, okay then.*

It was a tiny step on the road to becoming myself.

Chapter XXXIX. Protect & Survive

Third year had been a horrible, lonely time at school, which was not helped by a subject I enjoyed being destroyed by a teacher who hated me, so I was very much relieved to have a new English teacher for fourth year. Len Hughes was new to the school when I was put into his O'Grade English class. I did well in his classes, especially creative writing, and I was glad to get him again as my Higher English teacher the next year. It was in his classes that I was introduced to George Orwell, Aldous Huxley, and John Wyndham, author of my favourite novel, *The Day of the Triffids*. And then there was my first glorious reading of J.D. Salinger's *The Catcher in the Rye*. It exploded off the page. I didn't know books could be like that.

We also read a lot of poetry. I loved the bleakness of Sylvia Plath but it was another poem that destroyed me. To be more precise, it wasn't so much the poem, as the map Mr Huggins gave out along with it. The poem was "Your Attention Please" by Peter Porter, which reads as a formal radio announcement the public should prepare for imminent nuclear attack. Written in the 1960s, it was even more relevant in the 1970s. We were still in the icy clasp of the Cold War and it would be almost a decade before the Berlin Wall came down.

The threat of nuclear war permeated our culture, peaking in the early 1980s. It was during this period that *When the Wind Blows*, Raymond Briggs' graphic novel about a nuclear attack on Britain, was published. The couple in the story were based on his parents and their domesticity lent a terrifying realism to the horrors of radiation sickness. *Threads*, a BBC drama about the effects of nuclear war on Sheffield, was broadcast, while on the news Michael Foot, leader of the Labour Party, was shown leading a massive CND (Campaign for Nuclear Disarmament) rally. The groundwork for all this was laid in the '70s with the British government's public information campaign, *Protect and Survive.*

My copy of the *Protect and Survive* booklet is dated 1976. It includes information about how to make an inner refuge in your house by using doors to construct a lean-to[46] (the futility of this was beautifully illustrated in Briggs' *When the Wind Blows*). The handbook goes on to inform the reader that, if caught outside without cover, you should lie down in a ditch with a jacket over your head. Yeah, that's going to do it.

We were immersed in the fear of nuclear warfare and my coping method was to imagine it was something that would happen to other people somewhere else. And then Mr Huggins handed out his maps. These were crude photocopies of an outline of Scotland with concentric circles radiating out from a point on the west coast. The circles mapped the blast zone in the event of the Faslane nuclear submarine base was targeted. The first circle was the fast blast epicentre of death and destruction. In the second zone, people would go blind if they looked at the flash and their skin might melt but they wouldn't die immediately. To my complete horror, Cumbernauld was in the third zone where there was little chance of immediate death or catastrophic injury, but everyone would eventually die of radiation poisoning.

The class discussed the outcomes in some detail, with most people agreeing it was better to be in Zone 1 and simply blasted from the face of the earth. I was aghast. I did not want to be nuked into a dust shadow, or have my skin dripping from my face, but neither did I want the prolonged death of radiation sickness where I'd be bleeding from every orifice. The thought of my hair and teeth falling out was bad, bleeding from any hole was terrifying, but bleeding from the eyes was what got me. There were no good zones! My nightmares commenced that night and the horror stayed with me my entire life, which I guess was the object of the exercise.

Fear of nuclear holocaust aside, I enjoyed my English lessons with Mr Huggins, but it was in the art department that I really found my feet. The transition into Marianne Mitchell's art class in third year had been a turning point. She recognised I had some talent and was incredibly supportive at a difficult

---

[46] Lean-to: a simple shelter or structure leaning against an existing wall.

time. Then she left and Neil MacRae became the department head. I didn't know him as a teacher but had witnessed him deliver a couple tongue lashings so sharp that if I'd been on the receiving end, I'd still be feeling the sting. One of his tirades was directed at the girl who pushed me on my first day at school, and, yes, it was extremely satisfying to see her verbally flayed. I don't know what she did but it must have been pretty bad because Mr MacRae was a generous teacher, inspiring and with a good sense of humour. He could be waspish but he was witty with it and that made him great fun to be around.

Since I was not inclined to give him lip, his art class was a safe place to be. There was freedom in art, freedom in drawing, freedom in creating. It was hard work and expectations were high, but I had the drive to push myself on, to do better, and I listened to what Mr MacRae had to say. Although I enjoyed English, it wasn't a place where you could go at lunchtime or break. It didn't exist outside of Mr Huggins being there, unlike the art class where your work had its own place. That room was like nowhere else in school.

While I had periods of respite in school, tensions at home increased, especially between my father and me. My dad was a Labour man to his core. In the car on the way to the seaside, we sang "*Bandiera Rossa*" (also known as "*Avanti Popola*" or "The Red Flag"). I felt happy in those moments, singing along with my mum and dad, laughing as they pelted out *bandiera rossa trionferà* in the front of the car, the mood jolly, no glowering from my dad or tight lips from my mum.

There's a line in the chorus that means "long live communism and freedom" but we lived in a totalitarian state under the dictatorship of my dad. It appeared a benign regime, full of caravan holidays and days out to the coast, not to mention all those Saturday afternoons when my mum was working as a store detective in Lewis's in Glasgow and my dad took my sister and me to the ice rink in Falkirk, freezing on the benches while we went in circles for hours. And as long as we toed Dad's line, it was a fairly benign dictatorship. The problems began when any of us got ideas of our own.

I rarely heard my parents arguing, but the chill aftermath permeated the house like a thick smog. This terrible, tight-lipped silence could go on for days. My dad was angry a lot of the time. Angry at life, maybe. Angry at me, certainly. Mealtimes were often hell and I preferred when he was on backshift so he wasn't home. But when he was in the right mood, he could be hysterically funny. Sometimes he did an impression of the movements he made at work. The same four movements all shift long, shift after shift, like an automaton. We howled with laughter and so did he, but he was frustrated. He was an intelligent man trapped in a repetitive job. No wonder he put so much of his energies into union work.

My father was born in Glasgow in the tenement flat above the Sarrie Heid on the Gallowgate. The pub, once frequented by Billy Connolly, is home to a poem hand-written by Rabbie Burns[47] and to the skull of Maggie, the last witch to be burned at the stake in Scotland. The Sarrie Heid was famous, or perhaps more accurately, infamous, for its lethal champagne cider, known as shammy.

From the Gallowgate, my father's family moved to Weir Street in Govan, where he grew up in the shadow of the shipyards. He'd go raking in the middens for luckies, and one of his favourite boyhood tricks was to dip a rope in a muddy puddle then swing it around to splatter the girls' dresses, but he could be a charmer when it suited. When he went into the chip shop to ask for a bag of scraps—bits of batter given away free or for a penny—the women behind the counter usually took a shine to him and slipped in a piece of fish. Similarly, when he went to the grocers to buy a bag of broken biscuits, the women always added a few whole biscuits.

At school, he passed his 11+ exam but refused to go to the academic school because he wanted to be with his pals. When he left school, he wanted to join the Royal Navy, but he was under-age and my grandad refused to sign the papers for him. This didn't quash his urge to go to sea and even although my mum begged him not to, soon after they were married, he joined the Merchant Navy. When she was expecting me, she went down to the docks in Glasgow to meet him off his ship,

---

[47] Scotland's national poet. His many works include "A Man's a Man For a' That", "Tam O'Shanter" & "Auld Lang Syne" based on an old folk song.

but when she asked for my dad by name, they eyed her heavily pregnant belly and said, *There's no-one by that name on this ship.* It turned out my dad told everyone he was called John.

He took me aboard his ship a couple times. I met his pal, Jimmy One Tooth, who had a pet seagull he taught to smoke. Once, when my dad was suffering from delirium tremens (DTs) after too much drink, he began hallucinating. He saw wee green men running around the engine room and Jimmy helped try to catch them.

After we moved to Cumbernauld, he said he was leaving the Merchant Navy. He loved being at sea so my mum didn't believe him, not even on the Friday he told her that he'd got a job, but, sure enough, the following Monday he started work at Thames Case, a corrugated packaging factory, and stayed there for the next 16 years, first on the factory floor, then as a forklift operator and then a foreman.

His union activities began in the Merchant Navy when he was the youngest member ever to be voted onto the executive of the National Union of Seamen, and in 1966 he was involved in organising strikes for better pay and working conditions. His union activities strengthened at Thames Case. He joined the Society of Graphical and Allied Trades (SOGAT) and became a shop steward. By all accounts, he was an excellent advocate for his fellow workers and, though often a thorn in management's side, he had a good working relationship with them.

For the longest time, I adored my dad and thought he knew everything about everything, and he didn't go out of his way to dissuade me from the notion. But as I started having a few ideas of my own, relations between us became fraught. Negotiation may have been something he practised at work, but, at home, he expected his word to be law. After one of our rows, he stormed from the kitchen as I stood with a knife in my hand, burning with rage and wanting to stab him.

Occasionally, his union pals and their wives came to the house and I always liked being around them because the mood was light with a lot of laughter. I was around nine the first time I encountered Bob Gillespie. I was playing in the living room when my dad came home with a man who burst into the room like Taz from the Warner Brothers cartoons. He eyed up the chocolate Easter eggs lined on the sideboard and swept them into his arms. *Ur these fur ma boyz?* My dad cracked up while I sat with my mouth hanging open and a dread fear that this man was going to whirlwind chocolate out of my life for good.

A decade on, I'd be sitting in a bar at Charing X with Bob, enjoying a G&T while I told him about being at art school and he told me about his boy being in a band. I knew loads of people in bands, so it didn't seem that big a deal. As it turned out, Bob's son was Bobby Gillespie, who went on to be the frontman of Primal Scream, so it was quite a big deal after all.

Bob was a case and a half and, once I got over my initial terror of him, I loved being in his company. When his doctor told him to lose weight and cut down on saturated fat, Bob asked the owner of his local chippy to switch to vegetable oil and the owner replied, *You want a fish and chips, you come to Luigi. You want an oil change, you go to the garage.*

I also had a lot of laughs with my dad. That's what made it so hard. If he'd been like a stick of Blackpool Rock candy with **bastard** written all the way through, it would have been easier to deal with than my internal conflict.

I was 11 years old the last time he gave me a leathering. I'd been minding my sister after school and we'd decided to put on a show for our parents, which basically meant dressing up and performing a few songs and skits. She said I'd been bossing her around. Maybe I had, I can't remember, but I had all the pressures of producing, directing and writing to deal with. The thing is my sister and I hardly ever fell out so, when we did, it was treated like a crime against humanity. With me being the oldest, I always got the brunt of the blame, even when my sister was being a little shit.

My dad grabbed hold of me for a spank and all I could think was that I had pubic hair and I was mortified that he might see and so I struggled and screamed to get away. The more fuss I kicked up, the madder he got until he lost it. He put me over his knees, pulled down my pants, and thrashed me. A while later when I told my mother about my embarrassment, she laughed at me. I was 11, I'd just been leathered by my dad and she thought my embarrassment was funny.

You can talk to your mother about anything.

They thought this violation of my body was acceptable because it was normalised by the culture. Every week I saw Minnie the Minx being thrashed by her father in *The Beano*. Hell, sometimes she was made to bend over so that she could be spanked by the man next door.

The thing is, the man who leathered me was the same man who sat by the ice rink and took me fishing at the canal, and who took me on all those trips to the cinema to see brilliant films like *Daleks' Invasion Earth 2150 A.D.*.

I loved my dad but there were times, many times, when I hated him, and my feelings were never discussed. While he continually wound up my granny by bringing up the story about her throwing the poker at him, I was never allowed to bring up our darker episodes. Instead, I had to swallow them whole and be grateful while I was at it.

Adding to my turmoil was the fact I was desperate to please him. I wanted him to be proud. I wanted his approval but there was a direct conflict between what pleased him and what made me happy. I struggled to reconcile my feelings. I couldn't articulate them. I was lost in an emotional fog and it was screwing me up.

Chapter XXXX.

Merry Fucking Christmas

The first Christmas I remember anything of was our first Christmas in Cumbernauld. My sister was just a few weeks old and I was four. My memories are snapshots: the punchy smell of wood from a new jigsaw. Everyone dancing in the living room. Uncle Eddie burning me with a cigarette. We were dancing and his cigarette caught me in the arm. Hurt like a bastard and there was a bit of a fuss with him apologising and me whining and my mum trying to sort me out.

Eddie was my mother's brother. One time my dad went to visit him and found him on his knees, praying in front of two Jehovah's Witnesses who'd come to the door. My dad pulled Eddie to his feet and threw out the Jehovah's Witnesses. My dad was assertive that way but Eddie seemed a gentle soul. He once gave me an orange and a half crown (old money). I took the orange to school for my play piece. I'd just broken through the peel when the bell rang and was still holding my orange when we filed into the TV room to watch an educational programme called *Daisy Daisy*.

I knew we weren't allowed to eat in class, and I knew Mrs MacIntyre was watching me, but I was sitting cross-legged on the floor, orange just a lick from my lips and I couldn't resist a quick nibble. Before I could take a second, the orange was binned and I was sent up to the classroom to sit by myself until the programme was over. Funny, the things you remember. My Uncle Eddie made an unhappy marriage and was still a young man when he died in a motorbike accident.

You know what it's like at Christmas. Somebody does something once and it's part of your Christmas tradition. The fake auntie and uncle came once and then we were stuck with them. I'd have preferred a festive fag burn on the arm to watching the fake uncle gnaw on a turkey leg year in year out, but we had other traditions. For instance, I liked being in bed with my sister after lights out and singing "Away in a Manger" to her in a really sad voice to make her cry for the baby Jesus and I enjoyed writing Christmas cards for my friends at school.

I revelled in my passive aggressive card allocation. The friends I liked were given cards of the baby Jesus. The next tier was photographs of snowy mountains, followed by glittery Victorian scenes then robins, Santas and snowmen. The friends I didn't like were given cards featuring baubles and candles. I also enjoyed a tin of toffees in my stocking every year that I could eat while reading my new *Oor Wullie* book or *The Beano Annual* and whatever else I'd been given.

Some years it was just the four of us family members plus that pair. I liked it better when we had other people in the mix. The Christmas of '79 was a classic when my granny and grandad spent Christmas Day with us. A few years before, my sister and I had been bought single beds and, instead of blankets, we now had ultra-modern continental quilts (duvets) with matching nylon covers. We discovered that if we rubbed our feet up and down under the covers really fast, we could make sparks. Amazing that we didn't spontaneously combust. A while after that, my sister was moved into the small spare room so we each had a room to ourselves.

Everyone was in good spirits, including my granny, who'd been getting stuck into the Johnny Walker. We sat down for dinner in a crush in the kitchen and I pulled a cracker toy with her. The sudden snap caught her by surprise and she slid under the table. We fished around a bit and managed to retrieve her and she was taken upstairs to my room for a wee lie down. A while later, my mum sent me up to check on her. I stuck my head into the room and spoke gently into the dark.

Granny, are you okay?

Fuck off, she replied.

Okay, Granny.

I fucked off and went back downstairs, barely able to breathe for laughing. A while later, my granny was rummaging in the hall cupboard. She emerged with the vacuum cleaner and the consensus was it was safer to just let her get on with it.

The thing was, my mum had been complaining to my dad for some time about the vacuum's broken tube but he'd been reluctant to spend money on a new one, which meant she had to hunch over when using it. When Granny discovered this, she unleashed a volley of top-notch swearing.

What the fuck is this? Fucking carry on. What is this, a house full of fucking midgets? Thus, my father was shamed into buying a new vacuum cleaner.

The last time I saw my granny was in 1993. She had cancer and was in hospital. She clutched onto my arm and told me she was dying, and then we just looked at each other and cried. I was hopelessly out of my depth. She spent her last days at my auntie's house in Govan. She was 69 when she died and the priest leading her funeral service got her name wrong.

Chapter XXXXI.

Kramer Vs. Kramer,
Gregory's Girl
& The Joy of Sex

After several years of having only one friend and knowing a few people who stopped others from pushing me around, I became friends with a group who lived in Abronhill, on the other side of town. Abronhill was built later than the neighbourhoods orbiting the toonie. It was like a satellite and, because it was that bit further away, it had its own small shopping centre. The kids from Abronhill who went to Greenfaulds had to be bussed in and the school run was infamous. You knew that if the Abronhill lot were late that there had been another riot on the bus.

The last and busiest stop for the school bus was Ash Road. If the bus was full, you'd have to wait for the normal service and were guaranteed to be late, so, when the bus pulled up at Ash, everyone tried to crush through the door. Random punches and the threat of asphyxiation were daily hazards, and so were eggs.

A crowd of kids frantically cramming to get on a bus made an easy target, but the eggs were not thrown into the crowd. They were cunningly lobbed against the side of the bus, just above the door. By this method, globs of raw yolk and albumen were guaranteed to drip onto the maximum number of people. When the bus left Ash, the thundering stamp of feet for the pure hell of it was an everyday occurrence. Sometimes, seats were set on fire or thrown out the back window and insults were lobbed as freely as eggs. In short, the Abronhill school bus was a zoo on wheels.

One day, a new driver cracked up on the homeward journey and yelled at his passengers, *Whoever is still on the bus after the next stop is going to the police station.* Cue a mad stampede to the front, where the surging weight of kids caused the floor to collapse so the road could be seen whizzing beneath.

On another homeward journey, a boy called Dougie was being noised up by another boy. The boy kept needling Dougie. Dougie was the sort who never took anything lightly but he surprised everyone by staying calm until his tormentor got off at his stop. While the tormentor was waiting for the bus to pull away, Dougie laid down on the back seat. As the bus moved off, he kicked the emergency door hard with both feet. With perfect timing, it flew open, bounced off his tormentor's face and slammed shut again. Everyone watched out the back window as the bully stood there, stunned, his nose bleeding.

Most of my new friends lived around Oak Road so I started hanging out there. Not long after, I was asked out by one of the boys in the group. He was the older brother of a boy in my year, 19 to my 15. I said okay because it seemed rude not to and, when I was going home, he walked me down to the bus stop where I received my first kiss.

I was a bit taken aback when he plunged right in but it went okay until he stuck his tongue in my mouth and I gagged. If he noticed, he was too polite to say and we ended up going out for several months. So there I was after all that social isolation with a group of friends and a boyfriend.

Our first proper date was a trip to Glasgow for a meal followed by a film. Until then, the highlight of my week had been wandering around Woolco on a Friday evening, so this was heady stuff. My wardrobe was limited so I went on my first proper date looking exactly the way I did when I was at school, hanging around the toonie, or watching telly.

We caught the bus into Glasgow and went to 51st State, Glasgow's first American-style diner. This was years before McDonalds appeared in Scotland and the whole burger/diner idea was really exciting, especially as they had booths. Wow, it was just like being in a movie. It became even more movie-esque when the waitress asked if we wanted cocktails. Beyond a few sips of the froth from my dad's lager and a glass of Pomagne at Christmas, I'd barely tasted alcohol. (Pomagne was sparkling cider with a cork that popped for that celebratory vibe.)

Rather than own up to my lack of sophistication, or, worse still, give away the fact I was underage, I ordered the only thing on the cocktail menu that looked familiar: Buck's Fizz. I may never have tasted it, but I knew what orange juice was. It sounded nice and it was. My boyfriend ordered steak while I dined on my first ever meal of burger and fries and then we went to the cinema to see Meryl Streep and Dustin Hoffman in the pointless whingefest[48] that is *Kramer vs. Kramer.*

A few weeks later, we decided to go to the chippy at Abronhill Shopping Centre for a can of juice. There was a crowd outside when we got there, mostly teenagers, some of whom I recognised from school. At no point did I wonder why they were there. All I knew was that this crowd stood between me and a can of Top Deck[49].

I wormed through the throng and wandered towards the chip shop. It was dawning on me there was something strange about the assembled mass but, before I could give it any more thought, a man yelled at me to get out of the way. The crowd joined in, booing and jeering at me, and it was only then I noticed the crowd was standing in a circle around the chip shop, and in the middle was the angry man, a boom microphone, and me. The angry man turned out to be Bill Forsyth, the director of *Gregory's Girl.*

Gregory's Girl was the most exciting thing ever to happen in Cumbernauld and I knew nothing about it. At least, not until Bill Forsyth yelled at me.

There must have been a buzz about a film being shot in the town, especially one featuring local teenagers. At the very least, it merited a few words in the *Cumbernauld News*, but— despite flicking through the paper every week to see if anyone I knew was mentioned in the court roundup—the whole thing

---

[48] whingefest: a massive, never-ending moan (whinge).

[49] A low-alcohol soft drink marketed at kids! I can't believe they sold this. It came in flavours such as Lemonade Shandy (lemonade and beer), Limeade & Lager, and Cider Shandy. The alcohol content was 1.2% vol.

passed me by. I clearly didn't mix in the right circles, although by that point I did at least have a circle to mix with.

Several months later, while watching the film at the County, the air was ripe with an excitement that didn't let up the entire screening. Every time the audience saw someone they knew in the film, they shouted out and every time someone recognised a bit of the town, they shouted out. Since the entire film was shot in Cumbernauld with a bunch of extras, there was a chorus yelling at every scene. The cinema echoed to cries of, *That's my maw's hoose,* and *Check oot the toonie,* and, *What a wanker!* Where the film was edited to look like one part of Cumbernauld was next to a bit it wasn't in real life, there arose guffaws of laughter and bellows of indignation. Sad to say, my improvised walk-on never made the final cut.

I lasted a few more months with the boyfriend. We spent a lot of time in his bedroom, listening to *Bat Out of Hell* and studying the latest copy of *The Joy of Sex* magazine he subscribed to, which was illustrated with pencil drawings of a long-haired woman and a beardy man. The idea of sex was high on the agenda but we never went further than snogging and groping. He had a mobile disco and sometimes I went to gigs with him and got to be the DJ's girlfriend.

We were supposed to go see Rod Stewart but I ended it before the gig. I wasn't mad about Rod Stewart, he always just seemed like this old guy to me, and I wasn't that into the boyfriend. I'd only gone out with him because he'd asked and then it became something to do. My callousness would soon be rewarded with a broken heart. Karma, baby.

Chapter ☺ A Euphoria
XXXXII. Less Intense

Jobs that fitted around school hours were hard to come by. Paper rounds were so sought-after, they could be bought and sold and everything else was word of mouth. Somebody told me about a job selling rolls on a Sunday morning so I pitched up at the van and collected a tray to sell. I hefted it around houses, but nobody wanted to be knocked out of bed early on a Sunday, especially not the woman who stood, bleary-eyed, on the doorstep and said, *My man works at the City Bakeries, hen*[50]. I jacked it in after the second week, when the only rolls I sold were the pity dozen Dad bought from me.

Word got out I was looking for a job and Malky, not known for his kindness, surprised me, saying he was chucking in his job at Templeton's and it was mine if I wanted it.

Templeton's was a supermarket on the on the Seafar side of the toonie. Access was via a covered mall with skylights and white, moulded circular seats below for shoppers to sit on. These had a futuristic vibe and were known as the space seats. There was nothing futuristic about the dingy, nylon overall handed to me by the manager on my first shift. He was a small, fascist type who looked me up and down, contemptuous.

There were about half a dozen shelf-stackers, including Dougie, who never took anything lightly, and a serious boy from another school who sold the *Socialist Worker*. We congregated in the mall until the shift began at 5pm, when everyone made a mad dash upstairs to the manager's office. The scramble was not eagerness to begin work but to get hold of one of the two pricing guns that worked properly.

There were no bar codes or scanners, so every item in the supermarket was rung up manually by the checkout operator. A dud pricing gun meant a tedious shift picking off

---

[50] Hen: Generally, a term of endearment for women/girls. Found in various parts of Scotland but particularly common in Glasgow.

and sticking on labels, rather than the quick *chik chik chik* pricing of Smedley's processed peas.

The manager was a balding man with Brylcreemed hair, who wore glasses with thick, black frames and a grey dust coat over his suit. He was angry all the time, perhaps because he was constipated. I don't know for sure—I mean, we never talked about personal stuff—but he had that kind of look about him, as if hardened shit was building up inside him.

Dealing with after-school shelf-stackers brought his wrath to the fore and he seemed to find me particularly irksome. He tried venting his anger at me via heavy sarcasm, but just ended up more frustrated when I didn't care. He was just another angry man in a world of angry men. My dad, other people's dads, some of the teachers, men in the street, men in cars, everywhere these men, angry, angry, angry all the time and hating on life for it not working out the way they wanted.

The small manager in the grey dust coat clawed his way to the top of the supermarket pyramid only to discover the view wasn't so great. He was experiencing existential crisis, wondering, *What was the point of life?* Even though he concluded there wasn't any point, he still hated me for having all the pointlessness ahead of me.

He told me, *You don't even know you're born,* as he ordered me to the pet section. If he thought this was a punishment, he was very much mistaken. The cans were heavy and ridged on the top and bottom so they slotted into each other to be easily stacked, unlike tins of peas and carrots balanced on thin rims. In the tinned meats section, A&B Roll also came in ridged cans. The A and B stood for Aberdeen and Belfast, though what the roll was would forever remain a mystery to me. All I knew was it was a form of meat and the cans stacked just like dog food. Draw your own conclusions.

The assistant manager wore a white dust coat. He was a thin, pale man who reeked of desperation and, although he was not much older than me, he looked all done in, as if life had given him a good kicking then put the boot in again while he was down. Although he wore a shirt and tie, he never looked smart. He was unkempt in a shirttail-loose kind of way. He was the only person permitted to price and stack the sanitary towels and for that reason he was known as Dr White. He tried to be a boss, but no-one took him seriously, least of all his bovine-faced wife who worked on the cold meat counter, selling a variety of thinly sliced processed meats.

There were big slabs of corned beef, lumps of breadcrumbed ham and ham with no breadcrumbs, and something called haslet that looked like compressed scrapings. My favourite to look at because it struck me as odd the luncheon meat had a hard-boiled egg in the middle. The worst was the sliced tongue. I'd thought tongue was just a name and was horrified to discover it was an actual animal's tongue. *Jesus, who would want to eat that?*

She who sold the tongue and the haslet was reputed to have an affair with the butcher, a pink and fleshy man with a complexion reminiscent of the spam in her display.

For the stacking of shelves, I was paid £7.10 for seven hours work per week. From this, I put aside £5.00 each week for my art school fund. The remainder I spent on expressive clothes (no more plain skirts and dowdy shirts), used for bus fares, and buying Merrydown Cider at 90p per bottle. Wearing the green eyeshadow that transformed my appearance into that of an 18-year-old, I bought the cider at the off-sales counter in Templeton's and mostly I was served.

It's well-documented that low self-esteem, anger, and self-loathing are the results of childhood sexual abuse and this lucky bag of emotional turmoil commonly leads to risky behaviour and eating disorders. I didn't know diddly squat about it back then and, though I hate being predictable, I ended up ticking all the boxes. I was purging my body for years before I knew the word bulimia existed. Who knows, maybe I'd have gone down the self-destruct route anyway, but *Uncle* Allastair sure as hell took the chance to find out away from me.

Drinking was a salve for the hurt I'd internalised. It took the pain away and soothed my anger for a while, plus it made the world swim in a way I enjoyed. It was like going on a little holiday out of myself. I thought it might be nice to go to school drunk, that being pissed in chemistry would be quite pleasant. Probably a good thing that I didn't do it but still I wanted to escape my reality. I wanted to experience an altered state of awareness. I wanted to be altered.

I started going to the Orbit Youth Club in Abronhill. It was run by cool people and there was a heap of stuff you could do there, like playing tennis on a computer. Technology was new to us. Calculators had been around at school for a while but you weren't allowed to use them in maths, so we used the numbers to make words on the screen instead, *BOOBS, hELLO, hELLSBELLS.* Though it was exciting for us, the tennis game was just as blocky, with a white, square ball that moved really slowly across a dark screen.

There was a poster at the Orbit about the dangers of drugs. It listed substances and detailed the effects they caused. It was a handy guide, and although I never saw the attraction in sniffing glue, some of the items were very appealing and I used it to create a to-do list.

Cough mixture was not on the poster but, when a boy at school told me about how a certain kind could get you high and really trippy, I was most intrigued and hot-footed it up Boots the first chance I got. I swallowed it down then wandered the miles to Joe's in a psychedelic world that never looked so glorious. The trees were lovely. The bluebells were lovely. Even the lamp posts were lovely.

The cough mixture contained an ingredient that produced a euphoria less intense than heroin, but a less intense euphoria was still euphoria. I felt mellow, happy, and light and everything was interesting to look at. I was probably a complete pain in the arse to be with, but Joe was very chill. Joe was always very chill.

Making friends with Joe was a bit like how it was when I was a little kid. That thing of doing something and another where kid joins in and, before you know it, you're spending a summer together, chipping away at a mound of mud. With Joe and me, it was art. The two of us were always in the art room so got talking and, pretty soon after that, we became pals.

Joe was one of the Abronhill kids. He lived on Larch, right next to the school where *Gregory's Girl* was filmed. The school had just been built when they did the filming and, even though it's decades past, it's still the new school in my head. In honour of the film, an attempt was made to reprieve it from the demolition squad but that failed and now it's gone. Far and beyond Cumbernauld, people have a lot of affection for *Gregory's Girl* but, for me, the enduring legacy of the film is seeing Joe's bedroom window in the background of football scenes and thinking about the times we hung out there, listening to the likes of The Clash, PIL, and Devo.

The first intake at the new school was the year below us. Like me, Joe spent his entire high school career at Greenfaulds and had an interesting first day. He was walking along a corridor when a big third year grabbed the hood on his snorkel[51]. He used it to pull Joe's head down then kneed him in the face. While Joe was still reeling, the big boy laughed and walked on, the assault having barely broke his stride. After that, Joe made a point of befriending a boy in his class whose big brother was the best fighter in school. Joe was smart that way. He was also smart enough to not do the kinds of things I was getting up to, probably because he didn't have the same drive for annihilation of self that I did.

My cough mixture experience was so good that I was compelled to repeat it, but a neighbour from along the road worked in Boots so I couldn't buy it too often without arousing suspicion, plus the law of diminishing returns came into play. With each bottle downed, the effects were less amazing than the time before. Each bottle also became more difficult to drink. The first one slipped down like soft ice cream. The second took a bit more effort and, by the fourth, I was trying not to gag. On top of this, there was all the palaver of getting the bottles out of the house without being discovered. I may have had my own room but there was no privacy at home. It became so that it wasn't worth the effort and so, for the time being, I stuck with underage drinking.

---

[51] Snorkel: a waterproof, zipped nylon jacket with a fake fur trim on the hood. When completely zipped, it forms a snorkel, so it looks like the kid is hidden in the depths of the jacket.

Chapter XXXXIII.

Accidental Rebel

During my time in Marianne Mitchell's art class, I began thinking about going to art school. The following year, Neil MacRae helped me work towards my goal.

Back then, the number of kids in Scotland going on to higher education was around 14%. Most left school after fourth year and went to work. No-one from my working-class family had ever gone on to higher education and the notion of my parents financially supporting me through four years of study was as laughable as the idea of four years of debt was terrifying. If it wasn't for the student grant system, even thinking about going wouldn't have been an option. As it was, all our tuition fees were paid and we were given enough of a grant to get by on. That grant was my lifeline.

The truth is I didn't even know I was applying for a degree course. Because no-one in our family had gone to university, gaining a degree wasn't in my consciousness. I didn't know what a degree was. I just wanted to go to art school to spend the next four years learning to draw.

The usual route of getting there was to study for the qualifications required in fifth year and then work on an entrance portfolio in sixth year, but I couldn't contemplate staying on at school any longer than I had to. Despite a few bright spots, it was crushing me.

I had a feeling of deep dread when I found out my Higher Maths teacher was going to be the angry man who threatened to tie my Mucky Pup around my neck. I thought he'd make my life hell, but it turned out he'd have had a hard time recognising his own hands. Though the class was relatively small, he didn't bother learning anyone's name, not even Simon's. Simon was the boy who was as pale as boiled cauliflower and couldn't feel pain. He was also very good at maths, which was convenient for the maths teacher who enjoyed a liquid lunch in the pub every Monday before our double period.

He'd come back from the pub and start working out an equation on the board, but he couldn't tell his algebra from his arose, so he'd chuck the chalk at Simon and tell him to do it. Most of the casually violent boys left school at the end of fourth year so nobody was testing Simon's pain threshold by this time and he enjoyed the chance to show off a bit. It sounds like it should have been funny but the teacher was shambolic and disinterested and it was just depressing.

I'd been a straight A maths student, but if he didn't give a shit—*sines, cosines, yaddah, yaddah*—then why should I? Who knows, maybe I'd already peaked at maths anyway. It sure as hell felt as though I'd peaked at school. Even more pressingly, I had to get away from home. The differences in outlook between my parents and me were becoming more marked and the atmosphere between us was tense.

There's a scene in *The Wild One* when Marlon Brando's biker character is asked what he's rebelling against and he answers, *Whatta ya got?* See, that wasn't me. I wasn't looking for things to rebel against. I didn't set out to defy my parents. I wanted to please them, but the way things were between us, I just couldn't help but rub them up the wrong way.

Everything about me riled them. They wanted me to be a square peg they could push into a square hole. They wanted that I should dress the way they wanted—*Why can't you dress nicely*—and do everything they told me, and just behave in a way they approved. The problem was, I wasn't a square, or even a rectangle, or a triangle or any other shape they could relate to. I was a squiggle and, every time they tried to push me in one direction, I'd be off squiggling in another. They could never accept I had my own set of beliefs. To me, it seems natural that children become separate entities unto themselves, but this was something my parents could not accept and so, instead of encouraging my ways, they constantly sought to reshape me. This came into especially sharp focus when I said I wanted to go to art school.

Art school was viewed a bit differently back then. It was seen as a bohemian thing to do, an act of non-conformist rebellion. I'd already confounded my parents when I began, as Mother put it, *To sprout brains. You were normal and then you had all these brains and we didn't know what to do with you.*

Now that she was used to the idea of me having those brains, it was important to her that I got a job with a proper job title like *teacher, bank clerk, civil servant*—something she could understand and be proud of. Above all, she wanted me to conform. She became especially infatuated with the idea of me joining the police. During one of our heated arguments, she went from suggesting it as an option to telling me it was what I had to do. I shouted back, *I don't want to be a pig!*

It was the most rebellious statement I'd ever uttered at home, and I flushed as soon as the words were out, but when I saw my dad smirk, I knew I'd got away with it. His attitude was born out of the police being the enemy on the picket lines. Not that he supported me going to art school. Aside from considering art irrelevant and a waste of time, my father thought I was taking the piss, doing it to spite them. What I viewed as a natural progression, they saw as defiance and did everything they could to stop me going, refusing to write me the cheque for 10 pounds I needed to submit my portfolio.

The row about that exploded just before I went to work. I stood outside Templeton's, trying to fight back the tears. Dougie, who never took anything lightly, asked me what was wrong, and I tried to tell him, but my throat was tight and the only words I got out were *I hate my dad.* It was enough. Dougie nodded and the look in his eyes told me he understood. Though I didn't know the details about his situation any more than he knew about mine, I knew he had his own world of shit to deal with. That wee bit of sympathy I got from him helped strengthen my resolve.

In those pre-internet days, paying my submission fee by cheque was the only option on offer so I told Mr MacRae that I didn't get on with my dad and was having a bit of bother at home and asked if he'd write the cheque and I could pay him the cash. This he agreed to do and so I managed to submit my work for consideration. A few weeks later, Mr MacRae went down to Thames Case to get some cardboard for an art project and the person he dealt with was my dad. *Your father's a lovely man,* he later told me. And so he was. Just not all the time.

Going to art school became more than something I was working towards. It was my escape route from home and I was hellbent on pulling my portfolio together. When I had a loss of confidence along the way, Mr MacRae was there for me.

Lorraine, if you don't go to art school, you'll regret it for the rest of your life.

Chapter XXXXIV.

There Is No Privacy

I was 16 going on 17 and curious about sex. I wanted to know what all the fuss was about, but I was in absolute terror of getting pregnant. Every part of the process—from having a person growing inside me then having to push it out of my vagina and then having to look after it—filled me with horror on a cinematic scale. I suspected I might not be normal because girls were supposed to think babies and small children were cute and I didn't, a fact underlined when I became embroiled in a babysitting circle organised by Dougie's girlfriend. It was a like being stuck in a Pinter play, with me and two little kids sitting in a tiny living room, locked in eternal silence.

No to babies, no to children, no to being pregnant, but yes to finding out what was sex all about. So I went to my doctor and said I wanted to go on the pill and he flat out said no. He didn't approve of me wanting to have sex. *Like what the fuck?* But I was resourceful so took myself off to the family planning clinic in Kildrum, where they checked my blood pressure and gave me a supply of contraceptive pills. This was all well and good, but I now had these little foil packets I had to hide because—even although I had quite the responsible attitude and even although I was of legal age and even although it was actually none of their business—I knew my parents would not like this move of mine and would be like the doctor times one-million in disapproval.

There was no privacy at home to the extent that if I was using the bathroom and my father wanted in, he'd bang on the door. *Are you done in there? How long are you going to be?* Then he'd sit on the phone seat just outside the bathroom door and read the paper until I came out. It was excruciating. Nevertheless, I had to find somewhere to keep my pills and I found a hiding place among the books in my room. Although these books were only of interest to me, my mother found my little foil packets, which made me wonder if her fetish for housework was at such extreme that she felt obliged to dust between the pages she didn't read.

Having found my contraceptive pills, she did not say anything to me, but she did tell my father and very soon I became aware of a new tension among the many other tensions at home. My father silently *seeeeeeeeeeeeeeeeeethed* and my mother froze me out. When I was near her, she'd suck in her lips so tightly in disapproval that she was in danger of swallowing her own head. My father went from saying a friendly hello to the boys who called round for me to glowering at them and I had no idea why.

I'd gradually made more friends and these boys were my pals. We talked about music and politics and books and stuff on TV and how shit school was and how we wanted the world to be a different place. I wasn't sleeping with them. Not any of them. But instead of having a conversation with me, my parents assumed I was the Whore of Babylon, shagging every one of them.

They saved their anger and disappointment for quite a long time, letting the pressure properly build so, that when the eruption finally came, it was very nasty indeed. Shame was heaped upon me during the rant-fest and, for extra zing, my mother hit home with a belter. *That explains the weight you've piled on.* Not only did they think I was a slag, they thought I was a fat slag.

The one encounter I did have was with a boy a year older than me, who was similarly curious about sex. I barely knew him but we had a mutual acquaintance who brokered the deal. The act took place when the boy was home alone. We were in his single bed, orange streetlight streaming through the window and what occurred didn't amount to much more than a bit of rubbing. When it was over, I said, *Is that it?* Then I asked if we could do it again. I wanted to see if it was any better the second time around. He was young and able to comply, but it wasn't and I was left wondering what all the fuss was about. My next equally disappointing encounter would be well over a year later.

I spilled my teenage thoughts into my diary, the writing small, the lines packed close so that I could fit all my loving and loathing and angst and anger and fear and hope into the single page allocated for each day. These thoughts were not the sharing kind and it was important that what I wrote was the brutal, naked truth. I held nothing back, allowing the ink to give shape to my raw emotions.

The act of writing was a release and, when the diary page was full, I occasionally jotted down a few lines on the calendar beside my bedroom window. This turned out to be an utterly stupid move on my part but it did not occur to me that my father would go into my room and read my calendar.

He didn't like what he read but, rather than acknowledge these words were not meant for his eyes, he kept on reading. He flipped the pages with no sense at all that he had crossed a boundary. As far as he was concerned, this was his domain and there was no boundary to cross.

I was out when this happened and, by the time I got home, tension was crackling in the air and my mother's face was tight. *Your father is raging with you.*

I felt a quiver of fear and asked, *What have I done?*

He read your calendar.

My fear was replaced by horror. I flicked through the files in my mind, trying to recall how much of myself I'd given away. I remembered there was something about Ryan and me at a party. While I was trying to remember, I was also berating myself for writing it down, for writing anything down.

He wants to talk to you when he gets back from work.

For God's sake, I was thinking, it was just a bit of consensual snogging and groping.

I froze at my mother's next words.

He wants to see your diary.

Outwardly, I was immobile but, inside, everything was churning up so much that I could feel my heart pound in my guts. My stomach was flipping inside out and there was a tremor in my legs. *See my diary?* They'd be as well stripping me naked and marching me through the toonie.

My mother turned her back on me and I went upstairs to my room. My father was on backshift and wouldn't be home until 9 that night. I retrieved my diary from its hiding place behind my bookcase and went out to meet Joe. I told him I was in trouble at home but I was all screwed up about it and most of the words got caught up inside me, so he didn't really know what was going on, just that I was upset.

He walked with me to the railway bridge near Cumbernauld High. We stopped there and I opened my diary. I ripped out a page and tore it into tiny pieces and threw them over the side of the bridge. Joe watched as they fluttered like confetti onto the tracks. Page by page, I tore apart my thoughts and emotions. All the loving and loathing and angst and anger and fear and hope ended up in pieces on the railway line.

That night, I was called to the living room, where my parents were waiting to sit in judgement. My father had all day to lather up his rage and he was fuming. He had my calendar in his hand and demanded to see my diary.

I've ripped it up.

This didn't please him. He ordered me sit on the floor so he could thunder down on me as he went through everything I'd written, word by excruciating word. There were a few lines about the night two men in a van followed Maureen and me from street to street and how we had to run like hell to get away from them. I'd put the memory away in a box in the back of my mind, but now the fear of being caught by the men caught up with me and I started crying while my father rained down his ugly words.

What have you got to cry about? I've had enough of this. I've had enough of you. Your attitude is terrible. Are you trying to make a fool of me? It's about time you toed the line. Why can't you be more ladylike? What's wrong with you now? You like your friends more than you like us. What did you say? What did you say? Are you at it? Apologise to your mother for your behaviour.

SORRY SORRY SORRY SORRY SORRY SORRY SORRY
SORRY SORRY SORRY SORRY SORRY SORRY
SORRY SORRY SORRY SORRY SORRY
SORRY SORRY SORRY SORRY
SORRY SORRY SORRY
SORRY SORRY

SORRY

Your sister will get married before you. No husband will ever put up with you. YOU JUST WANT TO BE LOVED. It's about time you did as told. You're not going to art school. You're not going to art school. YOU'RE NOT GOING TO ART SCHOOL.

GET OUT OF MY SIGHT!

Never, not once, did it occur to him or my mother that I was entitled to my thoughts and a degree of privacy. They never asked about that night with the men in the van and if I was okay. They never ever asked me if I was okay. All I ever heard was *You're a disgrace* and *What's wrong with you?*

It was just as well they didn't know about the cough mixture or all the times I drank or the time I went to a party and spewed out of a bedroom window and watched my vomit trickle down the roof tiles into the gutter—a sight that made me laugh, which only served to underline that they were right, I really was a disgrace. And even although there wasn't much to know, it's just as well they didn't know about the time I dogged school with Ally.

It was a Monday afternoon, double maths with the disinterested teacher followed by a period of art history with Mrs Andrews. She was okay, but I was never going to be passionate about columns, no matter if they were Doric, Ionic or Corinthian. Besides, my mind had already been killed stone-dead by the double maths. Ally's house was empty, so we went there and played records in his room: *We're Only Making Plans for Nigel*. The next day in school, I was nabbed in the corridor by Mr MacRae.

Mrs Andrews said you weren't in class yesterday.

I agreed that I wasn't.

Were you dogging it?

I hadn't gone to the effort of making a back-up story and there didn't seem much point in lying but really, the truth was I didn't want to lie to him, so I said yes.

He smirked at me. *You never dog my classes.*

No, sir. I grinned back.

Okay, since you were honest, I'll let you off with it and square it with Mrs Andrews, but don't let it happen again.

I said I wouldn't and it wasn't a hard promise to keep for, once the novelty of not being in school wore off, it was a long afternoon. But still, it was best that my parents didn't know. Especially not about being in Ally's bedroom all afternoon with the house to ourselves. All we did was listen to music and chat, but because of the business with the pill and because I'd already come home with a badge (love bite) on my neck, and because of what they already thought of me anyway, assumptions would have been made.

The love bite was from a boy I was seeing who was a pal of Joe's. I tried to hide it with a scarf but my dad saw it and went berserk, saying I was never allowed out again. If he'd taken the time to speak at me instead of going full-scale nuclear, he'd have found out I didn't really like the badge and it wasn't something I was planning on doing again. He went berserk again when I got my ears pierced. It was nothing extreme or daring or alternative. Just a regular piercing of the lobes. I was 17 by then and it was just getting silly, but here we went again with how I'd upset my mother and how it was time I toed the line and *What is wrong with you?*

For years to come, I asked myself that same question:
What is wrong with me?
What is wrong with me?
What is wrong with me?
I never kept another diary until my daughter gifted me one in 2021. In fact, I stopped writing altogether. I hadn't yet learned to express myself through art, so everything became even more internalised. Something had to give and what gave was my skin. I began expressing myself through the medium of psoriasis.

Exam stress, parent stress, portfolio stress, life stress, stress stress, whatever-the-trigger, my skin erupted. It began with dry patches on my elbows that didn't go away. My doctor said I had psoriasis and gave me cream.

I told Maureen about my skin diagnosis and made light of it, but the cream didn't work, and I was worried. Maureen mocked my flaking skin. She was doing it to show off in front of Joe and I didn't like it. It was my skin. I could make jokes about it, but it wasn't on for her to do it at my expense.

She'd left school after fourth year and was going to hairdressing college in Glasgow and I was already uncomfortable about her visiting my cousin while she was there. It wasn't the going-to-see-him that was the problem. It was the digs she made about my auntie and uncle afterwards that I didn't like. Lately, there had been too many digs, too many sly comments. Her having a go about my skin angered me and was the start of a crumbling end to our friendship.

Meanwhile, the psoriasis spread from my elbows to my hands. Random strangers asked if I'd been in a fire. Random strangers can be wankers that way. I was hanging onto hope that the cream would work and didn't realise that I'd be living with psoriasis for the rest of my life. Some things you're better off not knowing.

Chapter XXXXV.

Into Each Life Some Rain Must Fall

Before I spent the afternoon dogging school with him, I spent several years exchanging glares with Ally. He lived in a three-storey house at the top of my road, but suddenly we weren't glaring any more. There was a crossroads on my route to school and, on a couple mornings, we happened to be there and fell into step. It turned out after all these years of hating each other, we liked each other after all. One day, Ally got there before me and waited and after that, we walked to school together every morning. Most days we walked home together as well, which meant we had over 300 conversations that year. Ally was waiting for me on the 8th of December in 1980. I must have been running late because I hadn't heard the news on the radio and so Ally told me that John Lennon had been shot dead. It was a real shock and we talked about it all the way to school, and, at school, people talked about it all day.

I spent my two years in Mr Huggins' English class, sitting beside a boy called Jimmy. His sense of humour cracked me up and for quite a long time, I was madly in love with him. We went out for a bit, but it didn't work at all, and Ally got exasperated when he had to act as a go-between for our exchange of Christmas presents. He gave me the Beatles' *Rarities* album that Jimmy had bought me, and I gave him Devo's *Are We Not Men?* album to give Jimmy. Even although I knew it wasn't working out, it still broke my heart when Jimmy ended it. Though it stung badly, we did manage to stay pals and once more lark around in our English class.

There was also Ewen, the Jam fan, with whom I spent a lot of time. He had a five-year plan for his hair so that he could have the same style as Paul Weller, though why it would take five years neither of us thought to ask. Ewen was with me when we dropped in at a party the fake uncle and auntie were having. We arrived just as everyone was doing their party piece. My mother's song was "Stormy Weather" and, after she'd done her turn and everyone had dried their eyes, they all started having a go at me. *Go on, go on, go on* until I gave in. It was funny to see their expressions change when I launched into Devo's "Jocko Homo". The room was pure tumbleweed and I revelled in the awkward silence. When we were walking downstairs afterwards, Ewen asked me, *What did you did that for?* It was impossible to explain and so I just laughed.

There was Kris the KISS fan and Andy the punk and Dougie who never let anything go. I went with him and Jimmy to see Toyah at the Glasgow Apollo. Before the gig, we stood on a waste-ground, sharing a quarter-bottle of whisky.

Ally, Andy and Jimmy were in a band with a boy from another school. I was their unofficial photographer and, when they went to a recording studio in Glasgow, they invited me. I finally had some sense of belonging. It felt good, but it was fleeting. Although I'd shared those 300-plus conversations with Ally, after leaving school, I never saw him again. I heard he joined the Merchant Navy and that's all she wrote.

I sat in my exams in various states of dismay. Maths was a blur, I walked out of the economics exam half an hour early and they asked questions in chemistry about things I swear I'd never heard of. Art was judged, not on a body of work, but on one piece created in a fixed period of time. The only exam that went smoothly was English but it was too late to change anything.

Joe had also applied to art school and we wanted to express our thanks to Mr MacRae, so chipped in to buy him the Vangelis soundtrack from *Chariots of Fire,* as it seemed like grown-up music and therefore a suitable gift for someone sophisticated. He looked amused when he opened it.

Industrial action meant there wouldn't be the customary evening disco for the end-of-year leavers. Instead, we had an afternoon disco in a disused dining hall, dancing in the daylight, surrounded by tables stacked with chairs. It was a bit shit, which was quite fitting.

I packed in my job at Templeton's in exchange for a full-time summer job in a photo processing shop in the toonie.

This sounded interesting until I discovered the films weren't developed in shop but sent away to Dundee to be processed. My job was filling in forms for customers and giving them a receipt. They returned with the receipt a few days later and I handed over their photographs. It was deadly dull but two of the three women I worked with were funny. The third was sour but it was marginally better than stacking canned peas. I opened a bank account and got a card, which allowed me to withdraw cash from a machine at a minimum of £1 a time. With all that money in my pocket, I could afford to go into Glasgow on my day off and buy a pair of roller boots.

Following on from the skateboarding craze of the late 1970s came the roller-skating craze of the early 1980s. Suddenly everybody was skating. Jimmy got into it big-style and I wanted to get into it too, so into Glasgow, I went. Lovely red and white, the boots were and, oh, how I loved them. My only skating experience had been at Falkirk Ice Rink when I mastered the art of going round in circles. My stopping technique had been to simply stop skating until I petered to a standstill or pelt into the sides and grab hold of the barrier.

My lack of prowess didn't curb my enthusiasm, not even when I gave myself a few bangs rattling around the playground of Ravenswood Primary. The tarmac was pretty bumpy and covered in bits of gravel that got into my skin when I fell. I needed a nice, smooth floor and what better place than the shiny, new Phase Four section of the toonie.

Phase Four was accessed via a high escalator or long, U-shaped ramp. I set off down the ramp, magnificently managing the tight turn as I whizzed past startled shoppers with next to zero control, then I enjoyed a brilliant scoot along the length of the mall and back before being apprehended by a security man and being told to never do it again.

Someone my dad knew from the Kingfisher pub had a son coming home from the army that summer. My dad and his dad set it up so that I met the son and, when I did, he asked me out. It was all a bit bloody embarrassing. I didn't want to go out with him but, instead of saying no thanks, I asked if he could roller-skate. He said yes so we arranged to go to the Barrowland roller-disco.

I had been a few times and, even though I still hadn't mastered going backwards, I was fairly proficient at going around in time to the music. He had a car and it was nice to drive in but it turned out that when he said yes about being able to roller-skate, he meant no. Compared to him, I was like James Caan in *Rollerball*. I don't think he enjoyed it much, even though he said he did. On the way home, he stopped for a fish supper and told me about the tour he'd just done in Northern Ireland. It sounded like he was pretty screwed up by it. Even though I felt bad for him, I wasn't up for a doorstep snog and so, when we got back and he moved in on me, I whipped him inside to say hello to my folks and then I ran away.

As well as splurging on the roller boots, I was able to buy clothes I liked. I never did get the Kickers French Jeans Boots that I craved after seeing them advertised at the County every week but at least there were no more sensible brown Derri boots. What I did get was a funky, wee yellow raincoat from a charity shop and some crazy, wild, baggy trousers that tapered at the ankle (this was years before MC Hammer—I was ahead of the game). I wore them walking over to Joe's and wee boys shouted at me in the street, *HAW, NEW ROMANTIC!*

I wasn't really a new romantic but one of the boys I worked with at Templeton's was into Spandau Ballet. I thought they were a bit silly and enjoyed arguing with him about them. We hung about a bit and his mum was delighted when I went to his house because she thought her son had a girlfriend, but we were just pals. It was a roasting-hot day and we were lounging in the garden when she called us in to see Lady Diana marry Prince Charles. Neither of us were interested so we stayed where we were, our jean-clad legs baking in the heat.

Walking about town, you'd often see **Lemo Mad Squad** spray-painted in the underpasses. The Lemo was Cumbernauld's most infamous gang and everybody knew somebody in it. In my case, it was the boyfriend of Maureen's big sister's friend of a friend. It was told to me in knowing terms that there was also a Tiny Lemo and I pictured miniature hooligans running amuck. The other tag often seen was **A.U.G.** in chunky, 3D effect. The letters stood for Abronhill

Urban Guerrillas. Although they were a common sight, I never heard of anyone knowing someone in the A.U.G..

I liked how **LEMO** and **A.U.G.** were always sprayed in the same styles, as though the gangs had corporate identities, but my favourite graffiti was sprayed on the railway bridge spanning the Vault Glen. Painted along one side of the grey, metal barriers, in letters two feet high was *INTO EACH LIFE SOME RAIN MUST FALL.* I saw those words a lot that summer when I was hanging out with Joe and going to parties thrown by boys he knew, who went to Cumbernauld High.

Simple Minds and U2 were popular bands in that circle, neither of whom I cared for. My Soft Cell album raised some eyebrows, but everyone agreed that The Clash's *Sandinista!* album wasn't very good. One sunny evening, I went for a stroll through Cumbernauld Park with one of Joe's pals and we recreated the dancing-on-your-back scene from *Gregory's Girl* under the same tree Clare Grogan and John Gordon Sinclair had lain. A few weeks later, that boy got a girl pregnant. They got married and moved into a house in the same road as his mum and married sister. When Joe told me, it sounded like that boy's life was over.

My Auntie Joanie died that summer. I called her Auntie Joanie, but she was my mother's aunt, so she was actually my great aunt. She lived in the Balornock area of Springburn, in an upstairs apartment of a four-in-the-block[52]. Her front door opened onto a steep flight of stairs that had whatever dog she had at the time, either barking or wagging its tail at the top.

Like my mother and her mother, Joanie was a small, slender woman but shrivelled with arthritis so appeared much older. Her face was like a wizened apple. Though incredibly wrinkled, her skin was soft, and she had an inner sparkle. My mum was close to her. We'd visit often, and Joanie also came out to us. She was stiff in the body and the arthritis twisted her fingers together like roots of a plant, but, after a couple martinis, she'd loosen off and be up singing and doing the

---

[52] Four-in-a-block: a common style of housing in Scotland with two apartments on the ground floor and two above (hence four-in-a-block), with each apartment having its own door leading directly outside.

Hokey Cokey. Even though she'd be paying for it the next day, her brief happiness was a joy to behold.

She was born during the First World War, in the mining community of Lower Valleyfield in South Fife. Her father, Alexander Gibson, was a private in the Royal Scots and a painter to trade. Her mother was my great grandmother who came to be known as Old Maw. She was a 27-year-old pit head[53] worker when Joanie was born. They weren't yet married, and Joanie is marked on the Fife registry of births as being illegitimate, which is a crappy way to mark a child's entry into the world.

In the few black-and-white photographs I have of her, she is a glamourous young woman. She enjoyed going out dancing but, although there was a young man in her life, she never got married. Her twenties coincided with the Second World War, so whoever he was and whatever kept them apart could have been war-related.

Her house was sparsely furnished but, when I visited with my mother and sister, we sat at the table by the window to have afternoon tea with China crockery and a proper teapot The loose-leaf tea was served as though we were in a fancy hotel. Her arthritis made life a chore and my parents invited her to come live with us, but Joanie declined, saying she wanted to keep her independence.

She was only 64 when she was found in her bed by her neighbour, having died peacefully in her sleep. I was told the news by my mother, then cut out of the discussion, and I wasn't allowed to attend her funeral. This was my mum's grief and there was no sharing of it. I think Joanie's funeral was the last time my mum saw her own mother. The neighbour took in Joanie's cat, and we inherited her dog, Toby, a gentle, collie who was slowly driven mad by the daily explosions from Croy quarry that echoed over Ravenswood.

A couple months after Joanie died, the brown envelope containing my exam results was posted through the door. I had a conditional offer of acceptance for art school and so everything hinged on the contents of this brown envelope.

---

[53] Pit head: the top of a mine shaft

Chapter XXXXVI. **Reflections**

When I was wee, they called me a daddy's girl. They said I was the spit of him. I never saw it, just like I never saw how much he looked like his mother or the way the shadow of my father's father was cast over his face. Now the three of them, father, grandmother, grandfather, crowd mine, jostling for position in the triangle between eyes and nose. I can't look at myself without seeing them. There's no space for my mother here. She busies herself elsewhere, catching me unawares when I hear myself repeating phrases of hers from long ago.

My Lithuanian heritage was no more than a story told to me by my grandfather, a sketchy story at that. It seemed far removed from me but, now that I see my grandfather in my face, I think perhaps his parents are there too and suddenly it seems very close. It's there in the mirror, looking back at me. If I've inherited their looks, is it possible that I inherited their sense of being out of place? It's a fanciful notion but one that helps explain why I grew up feeling I didn't belong.

I said before that growing up is not a linear thing and neither it is. Growing up is messy, full of complex strands and layers, and it's an eternal process. I got the grades I needed and thought going to art school was going to be the answer to everything, that, as well as being my escape route from home, it would set me on a clear path to the future, but of course it didn't work out that way. Going to art school was just the first step. My time there was also messy, full of complex strands and layers and the path was never clear.

For a long time, I hated Cumbernauld. I resented being made to grow up there when it wasn't even a real place and I especially hated what happened to me there. My unhappiness coloured my view of the town. It was only while researching this book that I found a new perspective. The more I learned about my hometown, the more fascinated and impressed I was by the astounding vision and ambition for Cumbernauld. It even had its own artist-in-residence, Brian Miller, who created brilliant abstract murals and sculptures familiar to everyone who grew up there in those early years. I took them for granted. Like the concrete pipes and boulders I played on, they were just part of the landscape. Now, I think it's extraordinary that art was given such prominence, that it wasn't an afterthought but integral to the town. For the first time, I began to appreciate and be grateful for the decision my parents made in 1968 to move from a single end in a Glasgow tenement with a shared toilet to this modernist utopian vision.

Throughout the process of writing, researching, and revisiting the town after being absent for a long time, I began to see Cumbernauld in a new light. It wasn't all good. I was shocked to see how the neat, geometric Millcroft Road flats we lived in had deteriorated to ghetto conditions but, as I walked through McGregor Road and looked at the house where I did most of my growing up, I thought about how egalitarian my neighbourhood had been. Teachers, factory workers, university lecturers, office workers, shop assistants, cleaners, landscape gardeners—even professional footballers—all lived next door to each other. (Paul Wilson, who played for Celtic, lived in the row in front of us.)

While my school experience was pretty grim— bullying, sexual assault and casual violence aside—it wasn't as relentlessly awful as I led myself to believe. Okay, when I think about it again—*bullying, sexual assault and casual violence*—a lot of it was even worse than I thought, but the teachers weren't. A few notable monstrosities aside, they were mostly good people doing their best for us.

When I walked through the town centre, I did not see a carbuncle, but a magnificent brutalist masterpiece. In an ideal world, the vision for the town would have been fully realised. Back in the real world, the toonie is no longer the thriving hub of the town and plans are afoot to demolish it and create something called a civic space.

I was amused to see what had become of the statue commissioned for the opening of Phase Four in 1980. Much maligned at the time, it is a depressing depiction of a world-weary woman wearing a headscarf and carrying a bag of messages. It is called something uninspiring like Cumbernauld Shopper. Its sheer drabness captured nothing of the dynamic modernist vision for the New Town and it now stands outside Spoons, looking as though it has been fly-tipped there, like a stained mattress at the side of a road.

The town has a new symbol in the 10-metre-high Arria statue overlooking the A80. Nicknamed the Angel of the Nauld, the steel sculpture represents the Gaelic roots of the town's name, *Comar nan Allt*, the meeting of the waters. Commissioned as part of a project to generate civic pride in Cumbernauld, the statue was created by artist Andy Scott who draws parallels between the town and Dundee:

"Cumbernauld has always had its detractors and, much like Dundee 20 years ago, it is fashionable to decry the town."

The original vision and optimism for Cumbernauld was astounding and should be a cause for celebration. Beautiful, ugly, modernist and brutal, the new town was all these things, often all at the same time but its unique urban design should be a matter of pride, not denigration. That it is a place like no other should be embraced and lauded.

Some of the deepest, darkest times of my life have their roots in growing up in Cumbernauld. Although I have come to terms with most of them, growing as a person continues to be non-linear and messy, but I have finally found some peace within myself just as I have finally found a sense of belonging. Strangely enough, that sense of belonging in this new place is also in a place that was invented. Ullapool, the village now I reside, was built by the British Fisheries Society in 1788 to exploit the herring industry.

Having found my place in the present, I am more able to accept the role Cumbernauld has played in my past. Though the deepest darks were rooted there, they were shot through by the brightest lights. Whatever the future holds for it, the town has its own mythology, created by us, the first generation to grow up there. It is a real place after all.

Acknowledgments

An early version of this book was written from a stance of hating Cumbernauld. This resulted in almost 100,00 words of screaming rage. Although my rage was justified, it blinded me to the many good aspects of growing up in the New Town. Joining the Cumbernauld 70s Gang on Facebook helped bring those positives into focus. My appreciation is to Iain Bryce and Iain Mackenzie, who founded the group, and to its members who continually add to this rich archive of photographs and memories.

Thank you to Joan Michael and Clare O'Brien for reading that first draft of rage and helping me begin the process of creating something readable. For those interested in such things, almost half was dumped and all of it was rewritten several times. Tons more thanks are due to Jon Miller, who gave me copious notes after reading that early draft and who has been so encouraging and generous with his time throughout the process. He and Clare are great poets, check out their work if you get the chance.

Writing something so personal and brutally honest wasn't always easy. I am indebted to Charlie, Caroline and MK for their support. Love you always.

The team at Outcast Press has been brilliant. I am very grateful to Sebastian Vice and Paige Johnson for taking a chance on me and for the excellent communication throughout the process. Working with Paige and Loretta Pederson on the edits was a joy and I just love, love, love the cover design by Cody Sexton. Many thanks to all four for being so patient with my abundant notes and queries.

I'd also like to give a shout out to my fellow Outcast authors for being generally awesome. You guys are so talented. I'm chuffed to bits to be published alongside you.

Heartfelt thanks to 'Joe' for being such a great pal, then, now, and all points between.

And finally, thank you for reading *Modernist Dreams Brutalist Nightmares*.

Glossary of Scottish *&* British *Words*

airing cupboard: storeroom or pantry in the home housing the hot water tank. Used for drying off damp laundry.

balls: a game played by girls in which two rubber balls around the size of tennis balls are rhythmically bounced against a wall, often accompanied by a chant. The balls are thrown to the ground in such a way that they ricochet against the wall and come back to the thrower, *bounce, bounce, catch, bounce, bounce, catch.* While the first ball is on its way back, the second ball is thrown and so it goes round and around. Skilled players did tricks like bouncing the balls under a raised leg or behind their backs and would twirl around on the spot while both balls were in motion without missing a beat. I never saw anyone being taught balls; it was one of those things other girls seemed to instinctively know from around the age of five or six. After years of watching, I made my first successful attempt at balls when I was 12. Just as I was feeling quite pleased with myself, a boy mooched past and mocked me for playing balls at my age. Humiliated, my balls playing era ended 15 minutes after it began.

bangers: fireworks similar to US cherry bombs, but—while cherry bombs are round—bangers are cylindrical. Bangers have been banned in the UK since 1997.

beamer: a deep blush caused by embarrassment, a blush so deep it glows. The beamer intensifies when others notice and draw attention to it.

biscuit: generally speaking, a biscuit in the UK is what you would call a cookie in the US. The US cookie would be called a scone in the UK.

Blackpool Rock: a stick of mint-flavoured candy with the word Blackpool embedded through its length so it can be read all the way through. Traditional Blackpool Rock is pink on the outside, white inside, with Blackpool written in red candy. Blackpool is a seaside town on the northwest coast of England. Famous for its Tower and illuminations, the town was a popular holiday destination for Glaswegians for much of the 20th century.

blaes: hardened clay or shale that is crushed to cover the surface of a sports pitch. In Cumbernauld, the pitches were made of red blaes. Grass was for looking at—not playing on.

blag: to persuade someone in a clever or slightly dishonest way to allow you to do something. For example, convincing the cinema staff I was old enough to watch an X-rated film.

bondage trousers: punk attire of the late '70s as worn by the Sex Pistols, typically comprising drainpipe trousers, often black or tartan, decorated with zips, D-rings, chains, etc.

bonnet: the hood covering the front of the car (which usually contained the engine).

brogues: a type of low-heeled, sturdy shoe with distinctive decorative holes like Oxfords have. Brogues can be very stylish, but in the scenario that I mentioned them, they would be considered old-fashioned and frumpy. The word *brogue* is derived from the Gaelic for shoe, *bròg*.

brothel creepers: crepe-soled shoes with suede uppers, often in bright colours, favoured by teddy boys in the 1950s and punks in the 1970s.

Busy Lizzies: a type of bush-like house-hold plant with small pink flowers.

caravan: a mobile home (called an RV trailer or a trailer house in the US). In the UK, they basically come in two forms, one small enough to be towed by a car, typically used for camping holidays. The other type is much larger and is known as a static, because, once it's been sited, it ain't moving again. These can be used as permanent abodes or rented out for holidays. When we started going on caravan holidays in the 1970s, toilet and washing facilities were provided in an external block on the site. The dining table in the caravan often had to be collapsed to form a double bed and the room was divided by means of a curtain. As the years progressed, internal toilets and separate bedrooms with bunkbeds inside the caravan became the norm. The first time we had a caravan with a toilet, the room was so small, a knee space was cut in the wall to permit sitting on the pan.

chippy: a place where chips (known as fries in the US) can be bought to take away. If you're feeling flush, you can order a pickled onion or pickled egg to go with your chips for supper. These are kept in big jars on the counter. Standard chippy suppers in Scotland include black pudding, white pudding, haggis, and red sausage. Black pudding is a blood sausage containing oatmeal. White pudding is like black pudding but contains suet rather than blood. Haggis is a traditional Scottish dish made from sheep's liver, heart and lungs mixed with oatmeal and spices. These dishes were designed in ye olden days to ensure no part of the animal was wasted. Red sausage is an abomination containing the undefined animal parts you won't find in normal sausage. Even fully cooked, the innards of a red sausage remain unnaturally pink. Other popular suppers include chicken and pizza. Supper items are deep-fried in batter, although, in the case of pizza, batter is optional. If the pizza is battered, it's known as pizza crunch. The pizzas used in chippies are disks of dough with red and yellow stuff painted on top to simulate tomato sauce and cheese. What they are actually made of is as much a mystery as red sausage. While nothing in a chippy is healthy, pizza crunch is particularly lethal. Chips and suppers were traditionally wrapped in newspaper.

chips: deep-fried potatoes similar to fries in the US but chips tend to be much thicker and recognisably contain potato. They are not usually as crisp as fries and are sometimes soggy. In Glasgow, chips are eaten liberally doused with salt and malt vinegar. People in Edinburgh eat theirs with salt and sauce. They are heathens.

chuffed: very pleased in a lovely and thankful way.

corky: a game to see who can get the last draw (puff) of a cigarette, meaning the cigarette gets smoked right down to the filter (and sometimes beyond). I have no idea if anyone still plays this ridiculous game.

council house: housing owned and maintained by a local authority (council) and rented to tenants. In the 1980s, Prime Minister Margaret Thatcher brought in the right for tenants to buy. Many people took advantage of this so there is now a shortage in the UK of secure housing at affordable rents. My homes in Cumbernauld were council houses.

creche: a nursery for babies and pre-school children.

dog roses: a type of rose with an open blossom, native to Europe. In Cumbernauld the dog roses tended to be pink although they can be white.

dogging it: playing truant; being absent without leave from school; playing hooky.

drainpipes: very narrow, straight-legged trousers (like drainpipes). After many years of flared trousers, drainpipes became very popular in the late 1970s.

drouth: to have a drouth is to be fantastically thirsty. Typically a morning condition brought on by imbibing a fair amount of alcohol the previous night. Irn-bru is recommended to remedy the situation.

dunt: a forceful push or blow.

empire biscuit: two shortbread biscuits sandwiched together with jam, topped with white glacé icing and finished with a glacé cherry. Sometimes jelly sweets are used instead of a cherry but I don't think that should be allowed. Empire biscuits are very popular in Scotland.

fags: cigarettes.

fankled: caught up; knotted; tangled; in a right bloody mess.

fanny: vulva. Used to be considered quite coarse, now a mild insult and often used to describe foolish behaviour, as in *Jim was a right fanny last night*. Although the word denotes female genitalia, it is usually the male of the species that is called a fanny.

feartiness: timidity; to be feart is to be scared.

fern cake: a small tart made from sweet shortcrust pastry filled with jam, frangipane and white icing then decorated with a fern pattern made from melted chocolate. A Scottish delicacy.

firth: sea inlet - where the mouth of a river meets the sea, as in the Firth of Clyde. From the Norse *fjord*.

flies' graveyard: a stodgy sweet pastry filled with a rich mixture of currants and raisins, these being the 'flies'. Traditionally served as a pudding at school dinners.

fry: a traditional British cooked breakfast, these days also known as a Full Scottish, a Full English, a Full Cornish, etc. depending on where you are in the UK. There are regional variations, for example while a Full Scottish may contain a slice of fried haggis, you wouldn't get that anywhere else. Within Scotland there are further regional variations. At the time *Modernist Dreams Brutalist Nightmares* is set, a fry up in our house would typically contain Ayrshire back bacon, fried eggs, black pudding, possibly fruit pudding, tattie scones, and some form of sausage, either pork or beef links or square sausage, and occasionally a Scotch pancake. The whole ensemble would be served with tea or coffee and either toast or a morning roll (large, soft bread roll). As an alternative to a full fry, any of the items mentioned could also be served on a roll. Fruit pudding is a Scottish delicacy and is a bit of a weird one. It's a mix of oatmeal, suet, dried fruit and spices formed into the shape of a large sausage and sliced. It adds an odd sickly sweetness to the plate. Tattie scones, also known as tottie scones, or potato scones, are made from mashed potato and flour, rolled into thin circles then cut into four triangles and fried. They are utterly delicious. Square sausage, known in some parts of Scotland as Lorne sausage, is another traditional Scottish delicacy and is made from meat, rusk and spices. As implied by their name they come in a flat square shape which makes them perfect for a piece and sausage (a sausage sandwich) or a roll and sausage. Scotch pancakes (also known as drop scones) are a type of thick, fluffy pancake. Morning rolls vary in different parts of the country. A Glasgow roll is a very fine specimen having a fluffy interior and a chewy bottom. It is not a floury roll. Tomato sauce (ketchup) or brown sauce (a spicy mix including tomatoes and tamarind extract) are common accompaniments to a fry up.

fud: vulva. Like fanny, it can also be used as an insult for the male of the species as in, *Jaimie Maguire is a complete fud.*

fug: smog; smoke.

gammon steak: a thick slice of lean, salted and cured ham. Pink in colour, usually grilled or fried, often served with a pineapple ring or fried egg.

gonks: novelty toys with a furry texture and big, googly eyes. With a spherical body and flat, felt feet sticking out at the bottom, they vary in colour and accessories, such as hats. (One of mine had a tartan bunnet.)

hairy banjo: yet another word for vulva.

heid: head, pronounced *heed.*

jack it in: give it up.

janny: school caretaker, a diminutive of janitor. In those days the janny was a figure of authority.

jobby: Scottish word for a shite, crap, turd. Billy Connolly told a great story about a jobby that wouldn't flush away.

joined up writing: cursive handwriting.

jotter: school exercise/work book. Derives from *jot*, meaning to quickly write. We had a maths jotter, a news jotter, a writing jotter, and so on. For reasons that no-one has ever been able to understand, we were expected to take our jotters home and cover them with brown paper or wallpaper.

kerb: the stone edge of a pavement (sidewalk).

lark around: mess around, play, have a bit of fun.

loch: Scottish for lake. There is only one body of water in Scotland called a lake (Lake of Menteith), all others are known as Lochs. The most famous of these is Loch Ness, where the Loch Ness Monster is said to reside.

luckies: a good find in an unexpected place such as a midden.

lumber: to get a lumber is to make a romantic or sexual connection with someone. *Did ye get a lumber last night?* Meaning, did you meet anyone?

manky: dirty.

mee-maws: the noise an ambulance, police car, or fire engine makes. *Mee-maw-mee-maw-mee-maw*, etc. etc.

midden: an area for disposing of waste. Tenement middens were in the back courts (at the back of the buildings). A midge raker is someone who sifts through the rubbish in a midden looking for luckies.

mince: ground beef.

mince and tatties: ground beef browned then simmered with onion, carrot, an Oxo cube and plenty of salt and pepper. Served with mashed potatoes (tatties or totties), accompanied by peas. I've heard tell that in certain parts of Scotland the tatties are not mashed. Forgive them for they know not what they do.

mither: to pester or make a fuss.

nark: to go on at; to cause annoyance.

news jotter: a school workbook for recording the news of the day. Entries from my primary 2 (age 6) news jotter include such riveting reading as *Last night Billy's Daddy brought him a lovely tartan tie*, and *To-day Elizabeth has on a new dark blue skirt. David has a new bike and it is bigger than Grant's one.*

nit nurse: a health official who periodically visited schools to check everyone's heads for lice and nits (lice eggs). We stood in long queues to have our heads investigated. Key areas were behind the ears and the nape of the neck.

outwith: a splendid Scottish word meaning outside or beyond. *It is outwith my control.*

pal around: to hang out together.

pan: toilet pan; toilet.

parallel trousers: a mid-1970s fashion, a sort of bridge between flared trousers (pants) and drainpipes. The line of the trousers ran straight down from the waist in parallel width, i.e. no taper and no flare.

pip: seed.

pissed: drunk; tipsy; inebriated.

plook: spot; blemish; pimple.

pokey hat: Italian hokey pokey men appeared on the streets of Glasgow (and of US cities) in the late nineteenth century. They rang bells and sold ice cream from push carts with signs on the side saying *Hokey Pokey*. A pokey hat is an ice-cream served in a pointed wafer cone.

pokes: a poke is a bag, as in a poke of crisps, a poke of chips, or a poke of sweeties. The word poke meaning a bag or sack dates from 14th century English. You can also poke someone, which means to jab them sharply with a finger or elbow.

post: mail.

pram: diminutive of perambulator; a child's pushchair or buggy.

prove: to allow the dough to rise when making bread.

pudding: a dish boiled in a bag, e.g. haggis (which was originally cooked in a sheep's stomach) or clootie dumpling, a sweet pudding made with dried fruits and boiled in a cloot (cloth). Also, a dessert with a thick, creamy consistency such as rice pudding. Also, a generic term for any dessert. The first line of Burns' poem *Address to a Haggis* is *Fair fa' your honest, sonsie face, Great Chieftain o' the Puddin-race*, meaning, Good luck to your honest, pleasant face.

pull a cracker: Christmas crackers, popular in the UK since the mid nineteenth century. Made of paper, usually bright and festive, they make a snapping sound when they are pulled and typically contain a paper hat, a small gift and a motto or joke. The jokes are traditionally the kind that elicit groans rather than laughter.

punters: customers.

ragman: Rag men (or rag-and-bone men) collect unwanted household goods from the street, which they sell to merchants. Traditionally this was done on foot or pony and cart, but, by the late 1960s, the rag men drove small vans.

rollers: big waves.

rounders: a game played by kids, similar to baseball but smaller in scale. The players score by running around bases.

scarper: to run away as fast as you can, probably because you're about to be caught doing something you shouldn't have been doing.

Scotch Broth: a traditional Scottish soup, thick and hearty— it's made to stick your ribs (metaphorically). Key ingredients are mutton (or beef) stock, root vegetables and barley.

scrappy: scrap merchant. Junkyard.

screaming ab-dabs: extreme anxiety or fear.

shag: to have sex; also a seabird.

shambolic: chaotic; a mess; disorganised.

shandy: a mix of lager and lemonade, very refreshing.

sherricking: a severe reprimand.

single end: a one-room tenement flat (apartment) with a bed recess and toilet on the landing shared by four households. Some single ends in Glasgow housed multi-generational families. People went to public baths for a weekly wash.

slag/slag off: to put someone or something down by using derogatory language; to mock or ridicule.

snib: a lock or latch on a door or window.

snogging: enthusiastic kissing; first base.

snooker: like a pool table but bigger, with complex rules.

sod: poor soul; a person to be pitied rather than condemned. A daft sod is someone who is a bit of a silly sausage.

stowed out: packed to the rafters; full; overcrowded.

swot: someone who enjoys learning which makes them a social pariah; an outcast. The opposite of a jock in a US school. Current term might be geek, but while there is geek chic there is no cool swot equivalent. More like swot grot.

take the piss: to tease; to mock; to ridicule.

teddy boy: 1950s rock 'n' roll fan, typically wore Edwardian drape jackets (Teddy derives from Edwardian), drainpipe trousers, brother creepers and bootlace ties. Hair would be slicked into a DA (duck's arse) or a Tony Curtis.

wanker: to wank means to masturbate; therefore, a wanker is a jerk, but wanker is a much stronger term. Alternative form is tosser. Having a toss also means to masturbate. Tosser is worse than jerk but not quite as bad as wanker. Only males can be called a wanker or a tosser.

zed-bed: a bed that is folded away during the day to make space. When folded it makes a compressed Z-shape.

Bibliography

1. Apollo: www.glasgowapollo.com

2. The Beano: The Beano Archives:
    https://archive.org/stream/TheBeano1974/

3. Bowers, Judith: Stan Laurel and Other Stars of the
    Panopticon; Birlinn 2007; ISBN 1-84158-617-X

4. Britannia Panopticon: www.britanniapanopticon.org/

5. BBC Archive on 4: The Three Day Week,
    www.bbc.co.uk/programmes/b03mcklz

6. BBC news website: www.bbc.co.uk/news

7. Cinema Treasures: www.cinematreasures.org

8. Civic Room: Lithuanian Research Project
    (Lithuanians in Scotland), www.civicroom.com

9. Cumbernauld, Town for Tomorrow:
    www.youtube.com/watch?v=ty6hKOYCDs0

10. Cumbernauld 70s Gang: Facebook private group.

11. Daily Record: www.dailyrecord.co.uk/news/local-
    news/pictures-world-war-ii-bombing-2307970

12. Gambaccini, Rice & Rice: British Hit Singles 9th
    edition; Guiness Publishing 1993; ISBN 0-85112-
    526-3

13. Glasgow City Council: www.glasgow.gov.uk

14. Glasgow Evening Times, 22nd June 1979.

15. It's Called Cumbernauld: www.its-called-
    cumbernauld.com/angel-of-the-nauld.shtml

16. The Glasgow Story: www.theglasgowstory.com

17. The Herald: www.heraldscotland.com

18. The History Vault: www.thehistoryvault.co.uk

19. Lost Glasgow, www.lostglasgow.scot/

20. National Health Service: www.nhs.uk

21. Scotland's People: www.scotlandspeople.gov.uk

22. Project Britain, British Life & Culture:
www.projectbritain.com

23. The Scotland Guide: www.scotland-guide.co.uk

24. The Scotsman: www.scotsman.com

25. The Summerland Fire Disaster:
www.summerlandfiredisaster.co.uk/

26. Undiscovered Scotland:
www.undiscoveredscotland.co.uk

27. War History Online: www.warhistoryonline.com

28. The Workhouse, The Story of an Institution:
www.workhouses.org.uk

Thanks for reading! Find more transgressive fiction (poems, novels, anthologies) at: Outcast-Press.com

Twitter & Instagram: @OutcastPress

Facebook.com/OutcastPress1

GoFund.Me/074605e9 (Outcast-Press: Short Story Collection)

Amazon, Kindle, Walmart, Target, Barnes & Nobel

Email proof of your review to OutcastPressSubmissions@gmail.com & we'll mail you a free bookmark!

International travels and ayahuasca, oh my! A novel about friendship dragged through the Amazon jungle and spit out through the stars with the aid of decades, DMT, and well-meaning debauchery.

More From
Outcast Press

How would you feel if today was your last day on Earth? Lotus is the part of yourself you're afraid and ashamed by, all the bad thoughts you shove inside the darkest corner of your brain.

This 18-poem literary/visual arts collection explores death, sex, drugs, drinking, honesty, and the afterlife. With rock 'n' roll flare and an appreciation for nature, Austin Davis unravels everything from teenage degeneracy to the cosmos in under 50 pages.

ABOUT THE AUTHOR

LG Thomson is an author who specialises in compelling characters, gripping plots, and gallows humour. Thomson's novels include noir thriller *Boyle's Law* and pandemic thriller *Each New Morn*. Her writing has appeared in a wide range of anthologies and literary publications, including *Wyldblood Magazine*, *Epoch Press*, and *Art North*.

Thomson now lives in Ullapool, a small fishing village on the northwest coast of Scotland, lying on the same latitude as Lost Cove, Alaska. To keep up to date with upcoming projects visit her website:

LGThomson.com

Twitter: @LGThomson1